CIPS STUDY MATTERS

DIPLOMA IN PROCUREMENT AND SUPPLY

REVISION NOTES

Sourcing in procurement and supply

Printed and distributed by:
The Chartered Institute of Purchasing & Supply, Easton House, Easton on the Hill, Stamford,
Lincolnshire PE9 3NZ
Tel: +44 (0) 1780 756 777
Fax: +44 (0) 1780 751 610
Email: info@cips.org
Website: www.cips.org

First edition October 2012

Contents

Preface

Welcome to your Revision Notes.

Your Revision Notes are a summarised version of the material contained in your Course Book. If you find that the Revision Notes refer to material that you do not recollect clearly, you should refer back to the Course Book to refresh your memory.

There is space at the end of each chapter in your Revision Notes where you can enter your own notes for reference.

A note on style

Throughout your Study Packs you will find that we use the masculine form of personal pronouns. This convention is adopted purely for the sake of stylistic convenience – we just don't like saying 'he/she' all the time. Please don't think this reflects any kind of bias or prejudice.

October 2012

CHAPTER 1

The Sourcing Process

Strategic and tactical sourcing

The main stages of a generic procurement process may be depicted as a cycle, beginning with identifying a need, proceeding all the way through to contract and supplier management, and then beginning again.

Sourcing is that part of the process that is concerned with 'how and where services or products are obtained' (CIPS) or 'the process of identifying, selecting and developing suppliers'.

The term **'purchasing'** is used to refer to post-contract transactional aspects such as ordering, receipting and payment. (This is sometimes called the purchase-to-pay cycle or P2P cycle.) The terms **'supplier management'** and **'contract management'** are used to refer to post-contract aspects such as the development and performance management of vendors or contractors.

The procurement process incorporates:

- **Pre-contract-award stages**
- **Post-contract-award stages**

Sourcing can be carried out at two basic levels: tactical (or operational) and strategic. **Tactical** and **operational** sourcing processes are concerned with:

- Lower-level decisions relating to low-profit, low-risk and routine items
- The formulation of short-range decisions as to how specific supply requirements are to be met
- Clearly defined requirements and specifications, and transactional sourcing decisions.

Strategic sourcing processes are concerned with:

- Top-level, longer-term decisions relating to items with high profit or high supply risk
- The formulation of long-range, high-level decisions eg about procurement policies, the supplier base, supply chain relationships etc
- Developing a deep understanding of requirements and of the supply market and individual supplier drivers and capabilities.

Lysons & Farrington argue that 'the status and importance purchasing now has requires a transition from thinking of it as a purely tactical activity to seeing it as a strategic activity.'

The sourcing process

Strategic sourcing is a complex process, involving a number of staged, interrelated tasks.

- Identification of the requirement
- Sourcing plan
- Market analysis
- Pre-qualification of suppliers
- Evaluating supply offers and options
- Creation of contract or relationship

This is only the beginning of contract management and fulfilment, and potentially ongoing relationship development. Further processes include the delivery of the product or performance of the service; post-purchase performance evaluation; post-contract 'lessons management'; and whole life contract management and supplier relationship management.

Not every procurement will follow every stage of the generic sourcing process.

- If a procurement is a **straight re-buy** of items already sourced from a supplier, for example, it will not be necessary to establish a specification, survey and source the market etc.
- If it is a **modified re-buy**, in that some of the requirement has changed, the same supplier may be used.
- **New buys** are more likely to conform to the full sourcing process.

Where the item required is a standard or routine one, 'sourcing' may be largely by-passed. There may, however, be the need to source a new or non-standard product or service – or the buyer may simply wish to stay aware of potential alternative providers in the supply market.

The extent of this investigation must be proportionate to the importance and value of the item, and the potential risks involved in securing supply.

- For low-value, non-critical items, it may be sufficient to conduct desk-based research.
- For more important items, categorise suppliers as either **approved** or **preferred.**
- For critical inputs, more rigorous measurement is required.

The **Pareto principle** (or '80/20 rule') is a useful technique for identifying the activities that will leverage your time, effort and resources for the biggest benefits. This is interpreted as 80% of spend, risk or value residing in 20% of supplies or suppliers.

This form of segmentation can be used to separate the critical few suppliers from the trivial many.

Another tool for prioritising is provided by Peter Kraljic (1983). Kraljic developed a **procurement positioning matrix**, which seeks to map:

- The importance to the organisation of the item being purchased, *against*
- The complexity of the supply market.

At a strategic level, the Kraljic matrix is used to examine an organisation's procurement portfolio and its exposure to risk from supply disruption. It can also be seen as a tool for assessing what sourcing approaches are most appropriate for different types of procurements, and how a procurement function can add value by leveraging the potential of each.

- For *non-critical or routine items* (such as common stationery supplies), the focus will be on low-maintenance sourcing routines to reduce procurement costs.
- For *leverage items*, the sourcing priority will be to use the buying organisation's power in the market to secure best prices and terms, on a purely transactional basis.
- For *bottleneck items* the sourcing priority will be ensuring control over the continuity and security of supply.
- For *strategic items* there is likely to be mutual dependency and investment, and the sourcing focus will be on the total cost, security and competitiveness of supply.

Surveying and engaging the market

'Surveying the market' means identifying or locating suppliers that may potentially be able to supply the requirement. A number of sources of information may be consulted to identify and research potentially suitable suppliers.

Once an organisation has an established supply base, it will usually store information about existing, past and potential suppliers in a *supplier database* or purchasing information system.

Potentially interesting suppliers may be contacted by telephone or email to request a brochure or catalogue, a visit from the supplier's sales representative, or a visit by the buyer to the supplier (sometimes called a 'site visit').

Supplier appraisal and pre-qualification

For high priority procurements, a more formal, systematic approach to information gathering about the supplier may be required: 'supplier appraisal'. The purpose of **supplier appraisal, evaluation** or **pre-qualification** is to ensure that a potential supplier will be able to perform any contract or tender that it is awarded, to the required standard.

'Pre-qualification' is the definition and assessment of criteria for supplier 'suitability', so that only pre-screened suppliers with certain minimum standards of capability, capacity and compatibility are invited or considered for participation in a given sourcing process.

Pre-qualification involves two basic processes.

- The development of objective evaluation criteria
- The screening of potential suppliers against the defined criteria: for example, using a pre-qualification questionnaire (PQQ) or request for information (RFI).

Whether or not a separate stage for supplier pre-qualification, screening or shortlisting is applied, there will be a need to appraise or evaluate potential suppliers, in order to assess their capability and suitability, prior to entering into negotiation or other processes for supplier selection and contract award.

Supplier appraisal is time-consuming and costly, so it may not be required for all new suppliers (eg for one-off, standardised or low-value purchases). It will be particularly important, however, for strategic or non-standard items; for major high-value purchases ; for potential long-term partnership relations; for international sourcing and outsourcing; and for supplier development and quality management.

CIPS have recommended a four-stage approach to assessing suppliers, as part of the supplier selection process. 1) Plan and prepare; 2) Action and individual assessment; 3) Evaluate and report results; 4) Recommend and feed back.

Gathering and verifying supplier information

Information about suppliers may be acquired by various means.

- Self-appraisal questionnaires
- Financial appraisal
- Checking supplier accreditations
- References
- Work sampling
- Supplier audit (also called a site visit or capability survey)

Detailed questionnaires should be sent to the potential supplier for completion, posing a range of evaluation questions. Many firms use multi-page checklists. The answers are analysed by the buyer, and scored. The supplier can then be rated.

One source of information on suppliers is to solicit the opinion of their current or previous customers. One approach to this is to ask potential suppliers for the contact details of selected customers ('references') and to contact those customers to ask about their experience with the supplier ('taking up' the references).

One key way to appraise supplier quality, and/or to verify supplier quality claims, is to evaluate the products or services themselves. Where a potential supplier is accessible, the buyer may use a supplier audit or site visit. A **capability survey**, carried out as part of supplier audit, is designed to gather detailed information about the supplier's capabilities.

Following the appraisal process, one or more suppliers may be officially recognised as being able to meet the standards and requirements of the particular buyer, and therefore eligible for invitations to quote or tender for contracts: this is known as supplier approval.

Vendor performance management

'Supplier management' is an umbrella term for many aspects of sourcing, contract management and supplier relationship management. After the sourcing, selecting and contracting of suppliers, it remains the buyer's responsibility to maintain regular contact and

1

to monitor and resolve any issues or problems and, if necessary, motivate the supplier.

Incentives for suppliers to perform to the required standard, and/or to improve, are normally built into the contract and other performance management documents. The aim of such incentives is to motivate the supplier by offering increased profit, or some other desirable benefit, as a reward for improved performance or added value.

An alternative approach to encourage suppliers to meet performance expectations is to use the threat or fear of being penalised for non-compliance with expectations. While penalties support compliance with minimum standards of performance, they usually encourage only short-term improvements at best.

Reasons to put effort into the formal evaluation of supplier performance:

- Help identify the highest-quality and best-performing suppliers.
- Suggest how relationships with suppliers can (or need to be) enhanced to improve their performance (eg to evaluate the effectiveness of purchasing's supplier selection and contract management processes)
- Help ensure that suppliers live up to what was promised in their contracts
- Provide suppliers with an incentive to maintain and/or continuously improve performance levels
- Significantly improve supplier performance, by identifying problems which can be tracked and fixed, or areas in which support and development is needed.

There are a number of critical success factors in a supplier's performance that a buyer may want to evaluate, and a range of key performance indicators (KPIs) can be selected for each.

Performance and review may be carried out in various ways.

- *Continuous monitoring* may be possible in some contexts.
- Performance may be monitored at key stages of a process, project or contract.
- *Periodic reviews* are often used: examining results against defined measures or targets at regular or fixed intervals.
- *Post-completion reviews* are often used for projects and contracts, with the purpose of exchanging feedback and learning any lessons for the future.

Vendor rating is the measurement of supplier performance using agreed criteria such as price, quality and delivery among others. One common approach to vendor rating is based on the use of a *supplier performance evaluation form*: a checklist of key performance factors, against which purchasers assess the supplier's performance as good, satisfactory or unsatisfactory. Another approach is the *factor rating method*, which gives a quantified, numerical score for each key assessment factor.

OWN NOTES

CHAPTER 2

Sourcing Strategy

The supplier base

The **'supplier base'** is all the vendors that supply a given purchaser. Supplier bases are often described in terms of their size or range (broad, narrow, single-sourced); location (local, national, international or global); and characteristics (eg diversified or specialised).

One approach to managing supply risk is by having **more** potential suppliers **(multiple sourcing)** of a given item or category of purchases, pre-qualified and approved as being able to meet the buyer's requirements.

More commonly these days, however, strong collaborative supplier relationships are used to 'narrow supply', enabling purchases to be concentrated on a smaller group of developed and trusted supply partners. **Supplier base optimisation** (or rationalisation) is concerned with determining roughly how many suppliers the buying firm wants to do business with.

In order to develop this opportunity, existing suppliers will have to be evaluated on performance, cost, service, quality, volume of business and potential or compatibility for closer relationship. An approved or preferred supplier list will usually be drawn up, weeding out unnecessary suppliers.

At the very narrow end of the scale, a single supplier may be selected for the development of closer partnership relations or an 'exclusive supply' contract: an approach called **single sourcing**. Buyers now increasingly recognise that multiple sourcing is not the only way to minimise supply risk or secure competitive supply.

Many organisations prefer the option of sharing supply between two suppliers: an approach called **dual sourcing.** This enables the buyer to maximise the advantages of narrow supply – while managing the risks of over-dependency on a single supplier.

Supplier failure can have severe consequences, particularly if the organisation is tied into a single-sourcing agreement. The financial stability and risk factors of sole suppliers should be monitored closely, and highlighted in the supply chain risk management process.

Single-source and dual-source arrangements are generally accompanied by a strong emphasis on mutual commitment, co-investment and relationship building, sometimes identified as 'partnering' or 'partnership sourcing'. Contexts in which partnership may be most beneficial:

- Where the customer has a high spend with the supplier
- Where the customer faces high risk
- Where the product supplied is technically complex
- Where the product is vital and complex
- Where the supply market for the product is fast-changing
- In a restricted supply market, where there are few competent and reliable supplier firms – and closer relationships could therefore improve the security of supply.

'Partnering aims to transform short-term adversarial customer-supplier relationships focused on the use of purchasing power to secure lower prices and improved delivery into long-term co-operation based on mutual trust leading to quality, innovation and shared values.'

The term **'sole sourcing'** (as distinguished from 'single sourcing') refers to a situation in which there is only one supplier available in the supply market for a given procurement. The market may be dominated by a single supplier: a market structure known as a monopoly.

The main concern for buyers will be a monopoly supplier's absolute power in the market: there will be no opportunity for the buyer to take its business elsewhere. Another issue is that buyers may be unable to specify their exact supply requirements.

Different approaches to letting contracts

There are a number of different approaches to letting a purchase contract, depending on the type of purchase and company policy. The organisation may already have negotiated a **framework agreement** or standing contract with a supplier, to meet a requirement of a certain type. In such a case, the requirement will simply be notified to the pre-contracted supplier by a purchase or call-off order, on the pre-agreed terms.

Buyers may be authorised to make purchases up to a certain value from the **catalogues** of pre-approved suppliers: catalogue purchasing is often used for low-value purchases and routine supply replenishments,

The organisation may send an 'enquiry' to one or more shortlisted suppliers, in the form of a request for quotation (RFQ), a request for information (RFI) or request for proposal (RFP). It will then invite the supplier(s) to submit a proposal and price for the job. These may be evaluated:

- As a basis for negotiation of price and other terms with the supplier or suppliers
- On a competitive basis: eg the best value offer or proposal 'wins' the contract.

Negotiation may be the main approach by which contract terms are arrived at, or may be used in support of tendering.

In a contract negotiation, the buyer's main objectives may be as follows.

- To obtain a fair and reasonable price for the quantity and quality of goods specified
- To get the supplier to perform the contract on time
- To exert some control over the manner in which the contract is performed

- To persuade the supplier to give maximum co-operation to the buyer's company
- To develop a sound and continuing relationship with competent suppliers

Negotiation objectives should be ranked as high priority, medium priority or low priority. Most negotiations depend on concessions from both sides, and this ranking procedure will help negotiators to determine where they can best afford to give ground or make concessions (low priority objectives) and which areas are non-negotiable (high priority objectives).

There are two basic approaches to the negotiation of contract terms with suppliers: **distributive bargaining** and **integrative bargaining**.

The organisation may prefer to use a competitive bidding or tendering procedure, in which potential suppliers are issued with an invitation to tender (ITT), or an invitation to bid for a contract, with the buyer intending to choose the supplier submitting the best proposal.

Competitive tendering is compulsory in the UK public sector, for example, for procurements by public bodies over a certain financial threshold, under the EU Public Procurement Directives (enacted in UK law by the Public Contracts Regulations 2006).

There are various approaches to tendering.

- **Open procedures** are open to any potential bidder on the basis of a widely advertised invitation to tender (eg in an open reverse e-auction).
- **Selective or restricted procedures** add a pre-tender qualification stage. Potential suppliers who respond to the tender advertisement are pre-qualified.
- **Restricted open procedures** involve inviting prospective suppliers to compete for a contract on an open basis, but the tender 'pool' is partly pre-qualified by restricting the advertising of the tender to selective media.
- **Negotiated procedures** involve the selection of a small number of suppliers to enter into direction negotiations with the buyer.

Intra-company trading

Intra-company trading refers to commercial relationships between entities which are part of the same organisation. One company, division or strategic business unit (SBU) in a large enterprise or conglomerate may supply goods or services to another.

The general purpose behind intra-company trading is:

- To support capacity utilisation in the supplying entity or unit
- To help the supplying entity or unit to cover its fixed costs in times of recession and low external orders
- To support the profitability of the supplying entity or unit
- To support the profitability of the group as a whole.

Intra-company trading policies may direct buyers to purchase selected items exclusively from internal suppliers. Alternatively they may require that buyers obtain quotations from internal suppliers, which will be competitively evaluated with quotations from external suppliers, and the order placed with the best value source (whether internal or external).

This highlights the key risk of intra-company trading, which is that internal supply may not be genuinely competitive with external supply.

A transfer price is an amount charged by one division to another within a single organisation. For example, we might have a manufacturing division and a sales division. The manufacturing division produces output which it transfers to the sales division at an agreed transfer price. This represents revenue to the manufacturing division and a cost to the sales division.

There are three main considerations for a firm when setting the transfer price for goods.
- Goal congruence
- Performance measurement
- Maintaining divisional autonomy

Other aspects of sourcing policy and strategy

The **make/do** or **buy** question: at one extreme, a firm could make its products entirely in-house, buying in perhaps nothing but raw materials: the value of the final product arises almost entirely from the work done by the firm. At the other extreme, a firm could minimise its own activities, buying in almost everything from outside suppliers or subcontractors.

The modern focus on 'core competencies' has led many companies to buy in products, components or assemblies previously produced in-house, and to **outsource** or **subcontract** a range of support functions and even core functions such as sales and customer service.

Key sourcing issues in outsourcing and subcontracting include:
- The need for the outsource decision to be based on clear objectives and measurable benefits, with a rigorous cost-benefit analysis
- The need for rigorous supplier selection
- Rigorous supplier contracting
- Clear and agreed service levels, standards and key performance indicators
- Consistent and rigorous monitoring of service delivery and quality
- Ongoing contract and supplier management
- Contract review, deriving lessons from the performance of the contract

Another important strand in sourcing strategy and policy is the question of whether to choose suppliers locally or internationally, and the **implications of international sourcing.**

Drivers for international sourcing:
- Improvements in transport technology
- Improvements in ICT
- Progressive reductions in trade barriers
- Sourcing efficiencies

- Country or region-specific supply factors
- Harmonisation of technical standards

One sourcing policy issue related to supplier relationship strategies is the extent to which the buying organisation is prepared to engage in supply **switching**. Buyers need to be aware that switching suppliers causes upheaval and cost.

If switching does take place, here are some key issues for buyers.

- The need for early flagging of contracts up for renewal
- The need for proactive transition planning and risk management

A **buying consortium** is a group of separate organisations that combine together for the purpose of procuring goods or services. A buying consortium might be created when a group of organisations see mutual benefit in aggregating their requirements: creating larger contracts, for economies of scale and increased bargaining power to secure advantageous terms. This might be especially beneficial if one organisation's requirements, on their own, are insufficient to attract attention – or discounts – from high-quality suppliers.

The consortium is represented in discussions with suppliers by a centralised or shared procurement unit, which may be the procurement function of one of the members, or a third party procurement service. The cost is shared by the consortium members.

Buying consortia can be found in both the public and the private sectors, but they are particularly encouraged in the public sector, in order to maximise value for money. In the UK, several local government authorities might form a consortium with a centralised buying unit. Similarly, there are buying consortia in parts of the automotive industry.

Benefits of consortium procurement:

- By means of enhanced bargaining power, the consortium can obtain discounts that would not be available to individual members – although there may be difficulties in allocating such discounts fairly among them.
- A consortium can establish framework agreements, simplifying purchase administration for members. This can lead to significant reductions in transaction and contracting costs, especially in the case of low-value items where the administrative cost is disproportionate to the purchase price of the items.
- Consortium members can pool expertise, knowledge and contacts, where these would be beneficial for particular procurement categories or exercises.

OWN NOTES

CHAPTER 3

Selection and Award Criteria

Selection and contract award

Contract award decisions are generally taken on the basis of a few objective, quantifiable (numerical) criteria – such as price or best value – which can be directly, unambiguously and consistently compared from one quotation or bid to another.

Criteria used for **supplier selection:**

* Focus on whether or not prospective suppliers are suitable, acceptable and capable of fulfilling requirements
* Are primarily *evaluative*
* May focus beyond any particular or immediate requirement, to the ongoing future supply needs of the organisation.

Criteria used for **contract award**:

* Focus on which supplier or bid is the 'best' option for the specific requirement
* Are primarily *comparative*
* Focus on the immediate requirement: the placing of a particular contract.

Organisations will formulate specific criteria to suit supplier selection:

* Their own **strategic priorities**
* Particular **process requirements** (eg for reverse logistics capability etc)
* Any **identified risk factors** in the sourcing situation
* Different **types of procurement**
* Different **supply relationships**

Supplier appraisal and selection models

It is worth learning Carter's 10Cs: refer to your Course Book. Another model for supplier appraisal is the FACE 2 FACE checklist.

The FACE 2 FACE model of supplier appraisal

Fixed assets Physical resources to meet buyer needs	**F**inancial stability For continuity of supply
Ability to deliver the goods Production capacity and reliability of delivery/ quality/service	**A**bility to work with the buyer Compatibility of culture, contacts, willingness to co-operate
Cost Competitive total acquisition costs, willingness to negotiate terms	**C**ommitment to quality Reliability of quality standards and systems, willingness to improve
Efficiency Use of resources, minimisation of waste	**E**nvironmental/ethical factors Policies and practices re CSR, ethics and environmental management

Selection criteria

Assessment of a supplier's financial position should be undertaken at an early stage. Financial status and stability are measured by the supplier's profitability, cashflow position, the assets it owns, the debts it owes, how its costs are structured and allocated.

Production capacity and technical capability refer to factors in the supplier's operational capacity and facilities, which act as indicators of its ability to fulfil the buyer's current and future requirements. The term 'production capacity' refers to how much volume the supplier will be able to handle, and how many units it can produce within a stated time period.

The supplier's development of, and adherence to, efficient systems and procedures for operation may embrace a number of criteria.

- *Compatibility* of the supplier's systems and procedures with those of the buyer
- *Willingness to comply* with any procedures, rules or systems specified by the buyer
- *Quality management systems*
- *IT development*: the potential for e-business and systems integration with the supplier

'Quality' will mean something different for the purchase of computer equipment, engineering components, building materials etc.

Ideally, a buyer would like to transfer as much of the cost and effort of quality management as possible to the supplier. The buyer will want to be assured that the supplier *itself* has robust **systems and procedures** in place for monitoring and managing the quality of its outputs.

Systems for the *detection and correction of defects* are known as **quality control**. This is an essentially reactive approach, focusing on: establishing specifications, standards and tolerances; inspecting delivered goods, often on a 'sampling' basis; identifying items that are defective or do not meet specification; and scrapping or re-working items that do not pass inspection.

Systems for the *prevention of defects* are known as **quality assurance**. This is a more proactive and integrated approach, building quality into every stage of the process from concept and specification onwards.

The term **quality management** is given to the various processes used to ensure that the right quality inputs and outputs are secured: that products and services are fit for purpose and conform to specification; and that continuous quality improvements are obtained over time. Quality management thus includes both quality control and quality assurance.

3

A **quality management system** is: 'A set of co-ordinated activities to direct and control an organisation in order to continually improve the effectiveness and efficiency of its performance'.

The importance of **environmental, ethical and responsibility** criteria in selecting suppliers has been highlighted by a number of high-profile cases, in which a buying organisation's reputation and brand have been damaged by the exposure of poor ethical, environmental or labour practice by their first – or even lower – tier suppliers.

A comprehensive definition of the term **'sustainability'** is sometimes called 'Profit, People and Planet' or 'Economics, Environment and Equity'. Sustainability may therefore be an umbrella term for a number of criteria related to issues such as the supplier's management of environmental impacts; sustainable resource consumption; compliance with environmental protection law and regulation; ethical trading and labour and employment practices; policies for corporate social responsibility and ethical conduct; and reputation management.

The prospective **supplier's upstream supply chain** (ie the supplier's suppliers) should be looked at as a supporting factor in its capacity to produce and its technical capability and as a supporting factor in its legal, ethical and environmental compliance.

Organisation culture ('the way we do things around here') is a reflection of the shared values, beliefs, assumptions and norms of behaviour that develop in an organisation over time. It is explicitly stated in corporate mission and values statements, but is also visible in the attitudes expressed by managers and staff, in their behaviour, in the 'look' of the premises, the neatness of staff uniforms. The culture of the supplier may simply be *incompatible* with that of the buyer: their values, or attitudes to quality, or tolerance for risk, say, may simply be too different to allow for collaboration or the management of expectations.

The identified costs of the proposed procurement will obviously be a key factor in evaluation of a potential supplier – although price may not be directly relevant at the pre-qualification stage. What the buyer will be interested in, however, is the structure of the supplier's costs, whether the supplier may be willing and able to commit to collaborative cost reduction initiatives, discounts and the total acquisition and ownership costs of the proposed purchase.

Award criteria

The main reason to distinguish between supplier selection or pre-qualification criteria and contract award criteria is the element of comparison or competition in contract award, in order to ensure competitive supply.

Competitive supply means the extent to which a supply arrangement provides supply which matches or exceeds requirements, at a cost which represents best value in relation to a given supply market. Contract award criteria therefore generally seek to balance technical criteria and commercial criteria.

Evaluating and verifying a supplier's technical capability and capacity may involve a complex range of factors, especially if the requirement and supply relationship is likely to be ongoing, committed and collaborative.

The use of specification as a basis for contract award raises several issues for buyers.

- Specifications must clearly, comprehensively and unambiguously set out exactly what the buyer's (and other key stakeholders') expectations and requirements are.
- Specification may be the best and last opportunity for buyers to build in qualitative, values-based criteria such as social or environmental sustainability or compatibility.

The buyer may exclude suppliers from bidding, or from contract award, if they fail to meet certain basic defined criteria in regard to suitability, financial standing and technical competence.

In relation to contract award in the public sector, only two criteria are allowable: lowest price or 'most economically advantageous tender'.

Lowest price is perhaps the most obvious, straightforward and easy to apply contract award criterion – once basic technical criteria (or more in-depth pre-qualification criteria) have been met. For routine purchases of goods to standardised technical specifications, lowest price is a simple test of value and competitive supply.

If 'best value' or 'economic advantage' criteria are used, the initial contract advertisement or invitations to quote should make this clear, and should explain the criteria that will be used to assess 'value' or 'economic advantage'.

Value criteria might include: quality, deliverability within target time scales, technical merit, innovation, risk sharing, health and safety or environmental performance. They should be directly relevant to the purpose and performance of the contract,.

Value for money is not about achieving the lowest purchase price: it has been defined as *'the optimum combination of whole life costs and quality.'*

'Best value' may therefore be defined as the lowest total acquisition cost which meets the purchaser's complex package of requirements.

OWN NOTES

OWN NOTES

CHAPTER 4

Supply Chain Perspectives

The supplier's perspective on sourcing

It is important for buyers to consider the supplier identification, appraisal and selection process from the supply market's perspective.

One key issue for the supply market in general is the accessibility of contracts and new business – especially to new, small or diverse (eg minority- or women-owned) suppliers. In the interests of corporate social responsibility, social sustainability *and* commercial advantage, buyers should consider increasing the accessibility of contracts to a wider supplier base.

It is necessary for buyers to:

- Appreciate the value of **widening and developing the supply market**
- Consider whether **sourcing policies and practices** may act as a barrier to participation
- Appreciate the **frustration** of suppliers unable to compete for business, and facilitate access where possible
- Appreciate the **ethical issues** in fair access to contracts.

Sometimes an appraisal arises because a **supplier** has asked to be added to an approved supplier list, or has expressed an interest in a selective tender. If the initial approach or request for pre-qualification comes from the **buyer**, the response from potential suppliers will not necessarily be favourable. There may be reluctance on the part of suppliers for various reasons.

A buyer should provide feedback to each supplier subjected to detailed pre-qualification or assessment. This will happen as a matter of course with the successful supplier, but even unsuccessful suppliers deserve to know how the buyer evaluated them.

The supplier preferencing model is an analysis tool which illustrates how attractive it is to a supplier to deal with a buyer, and the monetary value of the buyer's business to the supplier.

This is a useful model for sourcing and supplier management, because it shows that a buyer needs to maintain its 'attractive customer' status. There are various factors that might make suppliers keen to do business with a buying organisation, and therefore to present competitive offerings or bids: glamorous brand, fair and ethical behaviour etc.

Sourcing from SMEs and the third sector

Particular attention has been given to **small and medium enterprises** (SMEs) in recent years, because they are a significant contributor to economic activity.

- A 'micro' enterprise is one which has fewer than 10 employees and an annual turnover of less than 2 million euros.
- A 'small' enterprise is one which has 10–49 employees and an annual turnover of less than 10 million euros.
- A 'medium-sized' enterprise is one which has 50–249 employees and an annual turnover of less than 50 million euros.
- A 'large-scale' enterprise employs more than 250 employees, with an annual turnover of more than 50 million euros.

SME suppliers may have an advantage over large firms in clearly defined, small markets: it would not be worth large firms entering markets where there is no scope for economies of scale arising from mass production.

Issues when dealing with SME suppliers: the supplier's limited capacity to handle large-volume and aggregated contracts; the supplier's potential financial instability; and the ethical and business risk of a small supplier becoming overly dependent on a large customer.

If a buyer wishes to take advantage of these sources of value, for appropriate procurements, it may be able deliberately to prioritise, or give preference to, SME suppliers in its sourcing decisions (but not in the public sector).

Barriers to SME participation:

- Not being able to find out about opportunities.
- Lacking marketing resources to raise their profile in the supply market
- Believing that the process involved in bidding will be complex and costly
- Lacking expertise in areas such as interpreting complex requirements documentation or constructing good-quality proposals or tenders
- Lacking a track record of performance
- Lacking the capacity to handle large volume contracts.

The 'third sector' of an economy comprises non-governmental organisations (NGOs) which are operated on a not-for-profit (NFP) basis, generally reinvesting any 'surplus' from their activities to further social, environmental, cultural or other value-driven objectives. Organisations in the third sector have typically been set up to achieve a defined objective rather than to maximise profit. NFP organisations usually derive their funding from voluntary donations, legacies, sponsorships and government grants and subsidies.

Buyers in the public sector are perhaps most likely to source requirements from third sector organisations, as they source (or 'commission') the delivery of public services, such as education, health and aged care, leisure and arts services and so on.

Ethical sourcing

'**Ethics**' are a set of moral principles or values about what constitutes 'right' and 'wrong' behaviour. For individuals, these often reflect the assumptions and beliefs of the families, cultures and educational environment in which their ideas developed. Ethical, sustainable or responsible sourcing policies may cover a range of matters, depending on the ethical risks and issues raised by the organisation's activities and markets.

In addition to its own internal guidelines for ethical sourcing, trading and employment, a buying organisation may take responsibility for encouraging (or even insisting on) ethical employment and/or environmental practices in its suppliers. Sources of supply may be pre-qualified, for example, on the basis of basic principles such as non-use of child labour or forced labour, the paying of reasonable wages, the provision of adequate working conditions, health and safety, and the protection of workers' rights.

Supplier ethical policies and performance can be monitored by site visits and audits, to verify claims made on pre-qualification questionnaires. Where this is particularly difficult (eg with international or subcontracted suppliers), the buyer may use references, approved supplier or stockist lists and, where available, third party monitoring and certification services.

The **Ethical Trading Initiative** ETI is an alliance of companies, non-governmental organisations (NGOs) and trade union organisations committed to working together to identify and promote internationally-agreed principles of ethical trade and employment, and to monitor and verify the observance of ethics code provisions, as standards for ethical sourcing. The ETI publishes a code of labour practice (the 'base code') giving guidance on fundamental principles of ethical labour practices, based on international standards.

Fair Trade has developed into a worldwide concept, seeking to ensure decent living and working conditions for small-scale and economically disadvantaged producers and workers in developing countries. It involves an alliance of producers and importers, retailers, labelling and certifying organisations – and, of course, consumers willing to pursue ethical consumption by support for certified Fair Trade products.

One of the key principles of **business ethics** is the provision of fair, truthful and accurate information. This makes unethical the practice of deliberately inflating estimates of order sizes in order to obtain a price that would not be offered otherwise.

Another key ethical principle is protecting the **confidentiality of information**, where appropriate. Confidential information obtained in the course of supplier appraisal, for example, should not be disclosed without proper and specific authority.

A particularly important principle in ethical sourcing is what might be called '**fair dealing**'. A temptation to unfair dealing may be offered, for example, where:

- A supplier or potential supplier makes an error in a quotation or invoice, in the buyer's favour.

- There is potential to pay later than the payment terms agreed.
- Where quotations or tender bids are sought from suppliers where there is no intention to purchase.
- Where some vendors are favoured over others in a tender situation.

Another key principle in sourcing processes, which is often the subject of procurement ethical codes, is not offering or accepting gifts or **inducements** which may – or may be *perceived* to – influence the recipient's sourcing decisions. A related principle is that individuals should not make sourcing decisions (or divulge confidential information) for personal gain. Such situations create a **conflict of interest**, because the best interests of the firm or internal client conflicts with the personal interests of the individual.

Gifts and offers of **hospitality** are among the common courtesies of business dealings. The problem for procurement professionals is to decide when such practices amount to an attempt to induce a favourable sourcing or contract award decision, information disclosure or other favourable treatment.

The CIPS Code of Ethics is the ethical standard and disciplinary framework (the basis of best conduct) for procurement professionals in the area of procurement ethics. The code makes it clear that seeking membership of the Institute is in itself an undertaking to abide by ethical standards, and failure to do so may be dealt with by a disciplinary process.

Supply chain structures

The **process of sourcing requirements** from external suppliers is increasingly considered in relation to 'supply chains': as an issue of developing and managing flows of goods and value towards an end customer – not just as a series of one-to-one transactions or contractual relationships. 'The supply chain encompasses all organisations and activities associated with the flow and transformation of goods from the raw materials stage, through to the end user, as well as the associated information flows.'

This emphasises the need to:

- Co-ordinate activities across the supply chain
- Develop appropriate relationships with suppliers
- Structure supply chains effectively, in order to maintain control over their activities, while minimising the effort and cost of doing so
- Select, evaluate and develop suppliers in relation to the effectiveness of their *own* supply chain management
- Work collaboratively with supply chain members, to secure added value, cost and quality improvements throughout the supply chain as a whole.

Note the trade-offs between (a) the desire to minimise the costs and complexity of managing a large supplier base and (b) the desire to minimise the risks of having a very narrow supplier base. One of the solutions to these trade-offs lies in the way the supply chain is structured: specifically, in the development of supplier tiering.

The reasons for tiering of suppliers might be any of the following.

- The OEM wants to develop long-term relationships with key suppliers, but only has the time and resources to develop a limited number of such relationships.
- Standardisation of parts and variety reduction has reduced the number of parts required, so that the OEM needs fewer suppliers than in the past.
- There has been consolidation of suppliers within the supply market.

The impact of supply chain tiering on sourcing and supplier management in the top-level purchasing organisation or OEM may include the following.

- The sourcing, selection and contracting of the first-tier suppliers will be a crucial strategic exercise. It should involve a range of key stakeholders.
- There will be fewer commercial relationships to source and manage, so the procurement function can direct its attention to managing these key relationships.
- In order to minimise business and reputational risk, procurement staff will still need to 'drill down' through the tiers in the supply chain.
- The buyer may exercise influence over the first-tier supplier to adopt some of its own existing suppliers as subcontractors or lower-tier suppliers.
- Procurement may be freed up to pursue a more strategic focus.
- More and better supply chain improvements and innovations may be available.

Seeing the supply chain as a network is helpful for a number of reasons.

- It is a more strategic model for mapping and analysing supply chain relationships.
- It raises the possibility of a wider range of collaborations (eg buyer or supplier associations or consortia) which may offer mutual advantages.
- It recognises the potential of 'extended enterprises' and virtual organisations.
- It recognises that extended enterprises may overlap (with particular suppliers or customers in common), creating complex patterns of relationship, competition and potential risk (eg to information and intellectual property).

4

OWN NOTES

CHAPTER 5

Financial Appraisal of Suppliers

Why appraise suppliers' financial position?

The assessment of a supplier's financial position should be undertaken at an early stage in the sourcing process. If there are any doubts about financial stability or health, the supplier can then be eliminated from consideration.

Buyers need to appraise the financial position of their suppliers for two main reasons.

- They want to deal with suppliers who are financially *stable:* whose financial position is healthy. A supplier in financial difficulties cannot be counted on to fulfil a major supply contract.
- Buyers should seek to obtain prices which are fair to their own organisations and also fair to their suppliers. Negotiation of fair prices will revolve around the *costs* that a supplier must incur in providing the goods required – and its need to secure a reasonable *profit margin* to reinvest in the business.

A variety of financial tools are available for analysing the financial stability and strength of suppliers and competitors. Information for this analysis is available in the published financial statements of public, private and not-for-profit organisations.

Ratio analysis examines the relationship between sets of financial factors, expressed as a ratio or percentage. It defines performance indicators for organisations which can be *measured* using available financial data, and *compared* with performance in previous years (to highlight trends) or with other organisations (to highlight competitive strengths and weaknesses).

- Profitability ratios measure the extent to which a firm has traded profitably.
- Liquidity ratios measure the extent to which a firm is able to meet its liabilities or debts, both in the short term and in the medium-to-long term.
- Efficiency ratios measure the efficiency with which a firm utilises its assets
- Investment ratios measure the attractiveness of a firm to potential investors.

Sources of financial information on suppliers

Financial information about suppliers can be obtained from various sources.

- Their published financial statements
- Secondary data on markets and suppliers, eg from research agencies
- Credit rating companies
- Networking with other buyers who use the same suppliers
- Inviting the supplier's financial director to make a presentation

A supplier's financial accounts present only historical data, but supplemented by financial forecasting techniques (where appropriate) and comparison with the accounts of similar companies, they are a most useful source of information to the buyer.

Credit reporting and risk management agencies may offer a menu of services to businesses wishing to access credit and financial information about other businesses (such as suppliers).

Two main financial accounting statements of a company:

- The *balance sheet* is a statement of assets and liabilities at a point in time.
- The *profit and loss account* is a summary of income and expenditure over a period.

Financial terminology:

- An **asset** is something which is owned by the business and used in achieving business objectives. **Fixed assets** will be used in running the business for a long period of time (more than a single accounting year) and are typically of high value (land and buildings etc). **Current assets** move in and out of the business quite quickly (stocks, debtors etc).
- A **liability** (current or long-term) is a sum owed by the business to outsiders (eg amounts owing to trade creditors and outstanding loans, overdrafts, tax and wages).
- **Income** or **revenue** is amounts *earned* by the organisation eg from sales.
- **Expenditure** is amounts spent by the organisation. Capital expenditure is spending on items of long-term benefit (fixed assets) and operating expenditure is spending on items of short-term benefit.
- If income or revenue exceeds expenditure there is a *profit* for the accounting period; if expenditure exceeds income there is a *loss*.
- In order to survive, a business must have sufficient *cash* to pay its immediate liabilities. Being *profitable* does not necessarily mean that the business has sufficient cash resources. Firms need to ensure that they time incoming and outgoing cashflows: the process of **cashflow management**.
- **Working capital** is the company's net total of stock, debtors (amounts owed to it) and cash, *less* creditors (amounts owed by it). The circulation of working capital is a continuous cycle.

The financial accounts published by a limited company are usually a bulky document. Apart from the balance sheet and profit and loss account they will typically contain a number of other statements relating to the company's financial position. Here are some examples.

- A cashflow statement

- A five-year summary
- A chairman's statement

Earning profits does not necessarily guarantee a healthy cash position. This is a limitation of the profit and loss account: a business showing a healthy profit may still be financially unstable if the cash position is weak.

To overcome this shortcoming in the profit and loss account, company accounts include a further statement: the cashflow statement. This is designed to identify the sources of cash coming into the business and the ways in which it has been spent. The statement ends by showing the overall cash surplus or deficit at the beginning of the year, during the year, and at the end of the year.

5

OWN NOTES

CHAPTER 6

Ratio Analysis

Key measures of financial stability

Financial stability is a key criterion in the pre-qualification and selection of suppliers – as well as a key consideration in the management of ongoing supplier risk. Much of the information for assessing suppliers' financial stability will be gathered by surveying financial statements (and other available sources), and calculating *financial ratios*, which are used as measures of profitability, liquidity, gearing and investment.

As quantified measures, ratios give buyers a 'snapshot' of a supplier's financial position, and also facilitate comparison of the supplier's financial performance with:

- performance in previous years
- budgeted or planned performance in the current year
- the performance of similar businesses

Profit is the amount earned by a company once it has covered its costs of doing business.

Both buyers and suppliers seek to make a profit for a number of reasons.

- Profit means that the business has covered its costs and is not 'bleeding' money in losses.
- Profit belongs to the owners or shareholders of the business, as a return on their investment: a share of profits is paid to them in the form of a 'dividend' on their shares.
- Profits which are not paid to shareholders ('retained profits') are available for reinvestment in the development of the business, enabling it to acquire assets, meet long-term borrowings, update plant and equipment, and build up reserves.

Buyers must understand that suppliers are entitled to make a profit. This is important:

- To protect the security of supply
- To protect the quality of supply
- In the interests of corporate social responsibility.

Liquidity is key to a business. Being *profitable* does not necessarily mean that the business has sufficient cash resources available to meet its financial obligations when they fall due. For example, the profits may have been used to purchase 'non-liquid' assets (eg buildings, plant and machinery) which cannot easily be converted into cash at need. Or they may have been committed to shareholders, in the form of dividend payments.

The key point is that:

- A supplier must have sufficient *cash or 'liquid assets'* to meet its short-term debts and expenses and thus to maintain its operations and the flow of supply to its customers.
- A supplier must also demonstrate sound *cashflow management*: ensuring that it consistently times incoming and outgoing cashflows.

'Liquidity' is a measure of the extent to which a supplier is able to meet its liabilities or debts, both in the short term and in the medium-to-long term.

Gearing is a measure of the proportion of a business's long-term funding that is represented by long-term debt or loans – as opposed to share or equity capital. A business is said to be 'highly geared' if a high proportion of its funding comes from long-term debt. Gearing is relevant to the long-term liquidity (or solvency) and stability of a business.

- High gearing means that there is a lot of fixed-return capital in the overall financial structure of the company, which may be a risk factor in the long term: having to meet the regular interest costs of fixed-return loans may place strain on a company.
- Low gearing means that the company is relying mainly on equity capital, and should therefore have less difficulty in weathering difficult years.

Investment, in this context, is a measure of how attractive a business is to potential investors, based on the financial strength of the company and the likely return that can be expected.

A key tool in the analysis of all the above measures is the use of **financial ratios**. Ratios fall into several groups, the relevance of particular ratios depending on the purpose for which they are required.

- Profitability ratios – measuring the extent to which the business has traded profitably
- Liquidity and gearing ratios – measuring the extent to which the business has liquid assets sufficient to meet its short-term and long-term liabilities
- Investment ratios – measuring the strength and consistency of returns on investment delivered to shareholders and other investors.

Remember above all that the ratios are not an end in themselves. Examiners are interested in your ability to interpret and draw sourcing-related conclusions from information about prospective or current suppliers. Calculating a ratio is not the same as drawing a conclusion, but it can point you towards a conclusion. It is important to work carefully through the examples in the Course Book.

Ratios may highlight significant trends, but they do not in themselves provide reasons for the trends. To do this effectively, the interested party may need more information and a deeper insight into the affairs of the business.

Ratio analysis may be particularly helpful in highlighting:

- Significant comparisons **between suppliers**
- Significant **year-on-year trends**
- Significant **sources of supplier risk**

Profitability ratios measure the extent to which a business has traded profitably. Every business needs to generate sufficient sales revenue to cover its costs *and* pay a dividend to its shareholders *and* retain some profit as a reserve.

If a supplier is not showing consistent profits, the business may be in trouble, posing a supply risk. Alternatively, if the supplier is making large or increasing profits, a buyer may seek a price reduction.

6

OWN NOTES

CHAPTER 7

Surveying the Supply Market

Purchasing research

The procurement function must understand its supply markets. **Purchasing research** is 'the systematic study of all relevant factors which may affect the acquisition of goods and services, for the purpose of securing current and future requirements in such a way that the competitive position of the company is enhanced'.

The focus of purchasing research should include three basic aspects.

- **Demand analysis**. Standard procedures (such as Pareto analysis) should be operated to ensure that particular attention is paid to accurate demand forecasting for high-value, high-usage, high-risk materials.
- **Vendor analysis**. Buyers must evaluate the performance of current suppliers, as well as identifying, appraising and pre-qualifying potential suppliers.
- **Supply market analysis**. Buyers must appraise general supply conditions in the market, in relation to factors such as: likely availability and the risk of shortages or disruptions; market prices, price fluctuations and trends; and environmental factors affecting supply or demand.

Some of the questions purchasing research seeks to answer:

- What is the likely future demand level and usage rate of the item?
- How many suppliers are there in the supply market? Where are they based? Of what type and size are they?
- What new products, processes and technologies are developing in the market?
- What determines 'market price' for a given input?
- What threats and opportunities are presented by any or all of the above data?

The research into supply markets conducted by procurement departments is generally of an ongoing nature – involving constant market scanning and analysis.

Procurement staff must define the scope of the research work. If they identify trends with a potential to impact on the organisation a sensible next step might be to conduct a limited research project, perhaps by means of consultation with suppliers.

7

A buyer interested in the possibility of price changes in a certain material may be guided by any or all of the following factors.

- Historical trends
- Published price indices for the relevant industry or commodity
- Economic models
- Information from specialist price analysis and forecasting agencies

Basic supplier and supply market data can be used to support sourcing decisions:

- At a strategic level: eg in relation to make-do or buy, local or international sourcing, supply base optimisation or partnering decisions
- At a tactical level: eg in relation to supplier appraisal criteria, sourcing policies and methods, price targets, risk management or inventory policy
- At an operational level: eg in relation to negotiating strategies; the conduct of price negotiations, auctions and tenders; and supplier appraisal.

Responding to factors in the external purchasing environment:

- Emerging economic opportunities and threats, such as the opening up of new supply markets, falling or rising prices for critical supplies, etc
- Changes in social values, preferences and expectations, which may give rise to demand for new or modified products or business processes or higher expectations on the part of suppliers and other stakeholders
- Technological developments
- The trend towards globalised supply markets
- Constant amendments and additions to the law and regulation of business activities by the EU, national governments and other agencies

Demand analysis

Demand analysis provides essential data to enable buyers to source the 'right quantity' of items to meet the organisation's requirements.

The most important factors determining the size of the requirement to be sourced in a given situation are as follows.

- *Demand for the final product* into which the purchased materials and components are incorporated (dependent demand).
- *Demand for purchased finished items*, such as office equipment and supplies, computer hardware and software or maintenance services (independent demand).
- *The inventory policy of the organisation*: whether its main aim is to secure service levels by holding stocks or to minimise or eliminate stocks, to avoid the costs and risks associated with holding stock
- *The service level required*
- *Market conditions*, affecting the price and security of supply
- *Supply-side factors*, such as minimum order quantities and values

Many externally sourced items are subject to **dependent demand**: that is, demand for the item depends on the specification and production volume of a larger item of which it forms a part. Demand can thus be accurately measured on the basis of production schedules and materials requirements.

In order to avoid wasted costs of production, and operating losses, the organisation will want to produce a volume of outputs that is as close as possible to the volume it will be able to sell to customers. More often, however, the volume of production must be based on forecasts of market demand, or estimates of potential sales.

Other stock items will be subject to **independent demand**: not linked to production of another finished item. In the case of independent demand, forecasting will be based on estimating usage (and therefore replacement) rates.

The accuracy of **demand forecasting** is vital – but difficult to achieve. Forecasts are effective in certain areas, such as predicting stable demand, tracking sales trends, dealing with predictable seasonality, and projecting the effects of cyclical changes. They are not so effective in dynamic environments where demand and/or supply is erratic or chaotic.

Sources of information for forecasts:

- Historical data (eg on sales, or usage)
- Current data and information (such as that available from sales and production records, and suppliers)
- Market research and environmental monitoring

All forecasts require constant monitoring and revision in order to maximise and maintain their accuracy.

Various statistical techniques can be used to forecast market demand (sales) and/or independent demand (usage rates).

Statistical forecasting techniques

Simple moving average	This technique assumes that demand for a coming period will be 'average', that is an average of the demand recorded in recent past periods. So if sales (or usage) of a given item from January to June ran at 450, 190, 600, 600, 420 and 380 units respectively, we might anticipate that July's sales (or usage) would be an average of these six months: 2,640/6 = 440 units.
Weighted average (or exponential smoothing)	This technique recognises that older data is generally less reliable as a guide to the future than more recent data, and therefore gives extra weight to more recent data in calculating the average This adds some sophistication and accuracy by reflecting more recent trends, such as sales growth due to increasing customer awareness, promotional campaigns or competitor failure, or sales decline due to product obsolescence, say.

Continued . . .

Time series (trend) analysis	This method works by examining past data in chronological order, identifying underlying trends (consistent upward or downward movements over time) and projecting or 'extrapolating' these trends into the future. This is a more subjective, broad-brush approach. Historical data may show: • A *steady trend*: an increase or decline in demand, moving with a predictable pace that can easily be forecast • A *fluctuating trend*: rises or falls in demand are volatile or unstable, and reliable predictions are hard to achieve
Regression analysis	This method works by identifying connections or 'correlations' between certain measured variables (such as advertising spend, or price increases, and sales levels) and predicting the effect of changes in one variable (eg increasing advertising or lowering prices) on the other (hopefully, increased sales). This may involve complex modelling, and is often done using computerised spreadsheet or scenario analysis programmes.

Statistical methods are unlikely to be able to take into account all the various environmental factors which may cause fluctuations in demand. A number of more subjective or 'qualitative' methods may therefore be used:

• Marketing and/or customer research
• Expert opinion
• The Delphi method

Sources of market and supplier data

Supply market research is an essential process for gathering, analysing and evaluating data relating to businesses, markets and suppliers. The purpose of gathering such information is to achieve an optimal supply base to support developing business needs related to key performance factors such as cost, quality, delivery responsiveness etc.

Supply market research can be considered from both macro and micro perspectives. Obtaining market macro data and developing intelligence of the wider trends and opportunities is vital to ensure purchasing understand the relevance of these developments. Equally, the micro analysis that subsequently identifies specific suppliers and opportunities is essential to develop alternative business proposals.

Primary data are data collected especially for a particular purpose, directly from the relevant source eg customers, supply chain partners or industry analysts. Primary research is usually 'field research', involving surveys, interviews, questionnaires, observation or experiments.

Secondary data are data which have already been gathered and assembled for other purposes, general reference or publication. They are generally accessed by 'desk research'.

A middle course may be to buy in reports prepared by third parties, whether as commissioned primary research for another organisation (and then syndicated or released) or as a commercial service to industry data users.

A wide range of **specialist organisations** are engaged in providing market research and intelligence. Research industry associations and professional bodies sponsor a range of reliable websites to assist organisations in obtaining market research intelligence.

In economics, an 'index' (plural: 'indices') is a statistical measure of changes in a group of data. **Economic indices** are designed to track a nation's, or supply market's, stability and health, from a number of perspectives. For example:

- Stock market indices track the performance of selected companies in different stock markets
- Specialist indices also exist for other performance management criteria, such as sustainability, environmental responsibility, CSR and ethics.
- The Consumer Price Index (CPI) tracks variations in prices for a range of consumer goods and services over time, in a particular geographic location.

Primary commodities are items that occur in nature and provide raw materials for businesses to incorporate in their products. The main markets in which commodities are traded are in the United States. Major markets in the UK include the London Metal Exchange, with dealings in metals such as copper, zinc, tin and aluminium, and the International Petroleum Exchange.

Four groups participate in these markets: producers, buyers, traders, and speculators.

From a sourcing viewpoint, the main challenges of commodities are that they are unequally distributed, geographically: often, involving procurement in international sourcing and that they are subject to significant and unexpected fluctuations in price.

It is important for buyers continuously to monitor both relevant factors in commodity supply and trends and fluctuations in commodity prices. Buyers must try to minimise the effects of commodity price fluctuations – minimising the risk and cost of price rises, and seizing opportunities presented by price reductions.

Commodity markets also offer a number of methods to dampen price fluctuations and enable sensible forecasting and budgeting, notably 'futures contracts'. A futures contract is essentially the right to purchase or sell a specified quantity of a commodity in the market. Any price fluctuation that is bad for a *buyer* (ie the price has gone up) will equally *benefit* him as a *seller:* **'hedging'** the contract by making sure that the movement in price has a self-cancelling or off-setting effect on his financial position.

Supply market analysis

A useful starting point in the **analysis of supply markets** is to examine the main structural features that can be discerned. These are features that a buyer is unable to influence – the market has just developed in that way – but which may be an important influence on sourcing strategies and outcomes.

- The number of buyers in the market
- The number of suppliers in the market

- Methods of pricing in the market
- The degree of product differentiation in the market
- Technological developments in the market

A market may range from a state of **pure competition** (where many buyers and suppliers are active, and no one player is big enough to influence market prices by its actions) to a state of **monopoly** (a single supplier, who has a captive market and can effectively dictate a price to maximise its profits) or **monopsony** (a single buyer, who can effectively dictate the price it is willing to pay suppliers).

A buyer must be aware of these characteristics in its supply market, because they influence the strength of its negotiating position.

Market analysis is particularly important for procurements which are subject to instability. The analysis of a particular supply market as stable or unstable has an impact on sourcing strategies and tactics (eg the timing of purchases). If the supply market is unstable, there will be a much stronger emphasis on purchasing research, environmental monitoring, risk assessment and forecasting.

Forms of environmental scanning, strategic information gathering and analysis:

- Environmental audits and PESTLE analysis
- Industry analysis: one commonly used model for this kind of analysis is Porter's Five Forces model.
- Strengths, Weaknesses, Opportunities and Threats (SWOT) analysis and/or risk (likelihood and impact) analysis.
- Competitor analysis: monitoring and analysing the actions, strengths and weaknesses of key competitors and their supply chains
- Critical success factor analysis: examining what objectives must be achieved in order to secure competitive advantage for a supply chain in a given market
- Supply, demand and capacity forecasting
- Vendor analysis: evaluating the performance of current suppliers, and the capability and suitability of potential suppliers
- Market analysis: appraising general supply conditions in the market, in regard to supply factors, risks, pricing and pricing trends.

OWN NOTES

OWN NOTES

CHAPTER 8

Quotations and Tenders

Enquiries and quotations

Signalling a requirement to suppliers:

- For routine, low-value purchases or re-buys, there may be framework agreements or call-off contracts in place
- Reference to approved suppliers' catalogues or price lists
- For more modified, new, non-standard or high-value requirements, the buyer may have to initiate negotiations with, or solicit proposals from, suppliers
- An organisation may have different procedures in place for orders of different volume or value.

One approach is to send an enquiry, **'request for information', 'request for quotation' (RFQ) or 'request for proposal' (RFP)** to one or more suppliers.

Whether or not a formal tendering procedure is being used, it is common for a buyer to contact a number of suppliers in search of quotations.

A standard enquiry or RFQ form will typically set out the details of the requirement.

The buyer will then invite the supplier(s) to submit a proposal and price (a 'quotation') for the contract. Quotations may be evaluated:

- On a comparative or 'competitive bidding' basis
- As a basis for negotiation with a preferred supplier
- As a way of 'testing the market'.

There are ethical issues in the use of requests for quotation, which may be the subject of procurement ethical codes.

Suppliers will usually respond to the enquiry by supplying a quotation, representing their best price for supplying the buyer's stated requirements: a contractual offer.

Once the suppliers' quotations have been received, the buyer will need to **analyse** them to see which one provides the best value.

Other considerations, apart from price:

- Have all suppliers calculated their costs in the same way?
- Are all costs known – or is more information required?

- What is included in the different costings?
- Low pricing: is the supplier being competitive or compromising on quality?
- Is there a difference in credit period or payment terms?

Not all selection decisions will be as simple as a direct price competition. There may be differences in the specifications, differences in the level of support and /or differences between the buyer's standard terms and conditions and those quoted by the supplier.

There will be a wide range of factors (other than basic price) for the buyer to consider in evaluating the supplier quotations.

- Previous performance of the supplier
- Delivery lead time
- Add-on costs, running costs, and residual value and disposal costs
- Warranty terms
- Availability of spares and maintenance cover
- Risk of obsolescence, and ability to upgrade to higher specification
- Payment terms
- In the case of overseas suppliers, exchange rates, taxes and import duties.

In exceptional cases, there may be a **supplier 'cartel'**: collusion between suppliers, whereby they agree among themselves not to compete on price, keeping prices uncompetitively high. Such an agreement, being anti-competitive in nature, is illegal.

The tendering process

The organisation may prefer to use a more formalised **competitive bidding** or tendering procedure, in which pre-qualified suppliers are issued with an invitation to tender (ITT), or an invitation to bid for a contract, with the buyer intending to choose the supplier submitting the best proposal or the lowest price.

A full competitive bidding or tendering process may typically be required for contracts over a certain value threshold, in order to ensure the competitiveness of supply.

Tendering is the process by which suppliers are invited to put themselves forward (or 'bid') for a contract. There are several approaches to this.

- **Open tendering**, in which the invitation to tender is widely advertised and open to any potential bidder.
- **Selective tendering**, in which potential suppliers are pre-qualified (eg on the basis of their technical competence and financial standing) and 3–10 suppliers are shortlisted for invitation to tender.
- **Restricted open tenders**, in which prospective suppliers are invited to compete for a contract, but are partly pre-qualified by advertising of the tender being restricted

Pre-qualification of potential bidders on defined criteria provides a systematic means of eliminating suppliers that should not advance to the tendering stage. However, supplier appraisal and pre-qualification adds an extra layer of time and cost to the tender process and may not be required for standard, low-risk, low-value requirements.

A best-practice tender procedure would have the following steps.

- Preparation of detailed specifications and draft contract documents, setting out the requirement in detail
- Decision on whether to use open or selective/restricted tendering
- Determination of a realistic timetable for the tender process
- Advertisement of the requirement, tender procedures to be followed, and timetables for expression of interest or submission of bids
- Sending out of pre-qualification questionnaires (in a selective tender)
- Issue of invitation to tender (ITT) and tender documentation
- Specifications, and other tender documents, should be issued to each potential supplier in identical terms and by the same date.
- Submission of completed tenders or bids by potential suppliers
- Opening of tenders on the appointed date, in the presence of appointed officers. Tenders received after this date should be returned unopened. No tenders should be opened early.
- Logging of received tenders, with the main details of each listed on an analysis sheet or spreadsheet for ease of comparison.
- Analysis of each tender, according to the stated criteria, with a view to selecting the 'best offer'. This will usually be on a lowest-price or best value basis, but other criteria (such as environmental or social sustainability or innovation) may be taken into account
- Post-tender clarification, verification of supplier information, and/or negotiation, where required.
- Award of the contract, and advertisement or notification of the award
- 'De-briefing'

Assessment of suppliers' proposals

Tenders should be evaluated against the specific, objective award criteria set out in the initial invitation to tender. The general principle is that the successful tender will be the one with the lowest price or the 'most economically advantageous tender' (defined on the basis of whatever value criteria have been specified). However:

- The evaluation team may need to analyse whether and how effectively each bid meets the requirements of the specification.
- There may be considerable variety in the total solution 'package' being offered by bids: non-price criteria will have to be reviewed with particular care.

It will be important, therefore, for any invitation to tender to state clearly that:

- The buyer will *not* be bound to accept the lowest price quoted
- Post-tender negotiation may be entered into if necessary.

A weighted points system involves:

- The development of selection criteria (factors) and 'weights' (maximum ratings for each factor, as a proportion of the total decision).
- The assignment of numerical ratings or 'points' to each competing supplier, on each factor, based on the collective judgements of the tender evaluation team.

Sometimes it is not advisable to accept a supplier's tender without qualification or clarification. The possibility of **post-tender negotiations** (PTN) should be clearly flagged in the invitation to tender.

CIPS guidelines on PTN:

- Post-tender negotiation meetings should be conducted by at least two members of the purchasing organisation, to ensure transparency and accountability.
- The negotiators from the purchasing organisation should have cleared their proposed negotiating strategy with relevant managers.
- Notes of the meeting should be taken to ensure that a record is kept of the negotiations and conclusions.
- Buyers should conduct the negotiation in a professional and ethical manner.

The contract should now be formally recognised by issuing the relevant contract documentation. Typically, the components for the actual contract will be the invitation to tender, the supplier's written proposal, plus any modifications (as may have been agreed at a bid presentation or in the post-tender negotiation).

Where supply is switched from one supplier to another, or an existing contract is not renewed, successful tenderers should formally be asked to produce a plan showing how they propose to take over smoothly from existing suppliers.

Recommending sources of supply

The outcome of a competitive quotation or tender process may be a report from the procurement or tender evaluation team, recommending the supplier or bid which the team believes should be awarded the contract.

In less clear cut situations the procurement team may be required to:

- Submit a report, outlining and justifying the supplier appraisal and selection process, and recommending a shortlist of sources of supply, or a preferred supplier, for contract award.
- Present a business case for recommendation of a given supply approach, strategy or market for procurement policy makers
- Approve, prefer, confirm or certify suppliers for use by non-procurement buyers.

Preferred suppliers are a small number of suppliers with whom the buyer has a supply agreement.

Approved suppliers have been pre-qualified as satisfactory suppliers for one or more products or services.

Confirmed suppliers have been specifically requested by a user (eg design or production) and accepted by the procurement function.

A **SWOT analysis** is a strategic tool designed to appraise the overall state of an organisation and indicate areas for concern and areas for improvement. Here are some of the questions you might pose, depending on the information available.

STRENGTHS:	WEAKNESSES:
What are the strengths of the supplier (and/or this bid) compared with competitors? What unique resources and competencies can the supplier draw on? What resources are available to the supplier at lower cost than to other suppliers?	What aspects of the supplier's performance could be improved? What managerial, operational, technological or financial limitations constrain the activities of the supplier? Where is the supplier's bid weak, compared to competing bids?
OPPORTUNITIES:	THREATS:
Is this contract a significant opportunity for the supplier? What trends (eg technology development) is the supplier exploiting, or could the supplier exploit, in order to improve performance? How might this supplier contribute to opportunities for the whole supply chain?	What external trends or internal weaknesses expose the supplier (and supply chain) to risk? How well placed is the supplier to cope with technological, legal or other changes? Does the supplier have any significant financial problems or instabilities?

8

OWN NOTES

CHAPTER 9

E-sourcing Tools

E-procurement and e-sourcing

The internet is a worldwide computer network allowing computers to communicate via telecommunications links. The network can also be accessed from laptop computers and personal hand-held devices such as tablet and palm computers and 'smart' mobile phones.

E-commerce refers to business transactions carried out online via ICT – usually the internet. E-commerce has facilitated direct marketing, linking customers directly with suppliers across the whole value chain. It is a means of automating business transactions and workflows – and also streamlining and improving them.

Some websites exist only to provide information about products, services or other matters. They might provide contact details for would-be customers to make direct enquiries or orders, or to find a local retail outlet or distributor. A transaction-supporting website, however, can be a **'virtual'** retail outlet, warehouse, supermarket, auction room or market exchange.

For sourcing functions, the internet offers particular benefits.

- Wider choice of suppliers, including global and small suppliers, via the internet
- Savings in sourcing costs
- Support for low inventory and efficient stock turnover
- Improved supply chain relationships and coordination

CIPS defines **e-purchasing** as: 'the combined use of information and communication technology through electronic means to enhance external and internal purchasing and supply management processes.'

'E-sourcing' is defined by CIPS as 'using the internet to make decisions and form strategies regarding how and where services or products are obtained': in other words, using electronic tools for the sourcing process.

Major types of **e-sourcing tools:**

- E-catalogues: suppliers exhibit their products in electronic catalogues
- Supplier portals and market exchanges
- Online supplier evaluation data
- E-auctions
- E-tendering

9

Potential benefits of developing e-sourcing:

- Reduced costs through increased process efficiencies, reduced sourcing costs, improvements in contract performance management etc
- Best practice development
- Enhanced quality and capability
- Reduced sourcing cycle times
- Improved training and efficiency

Advantages of e-sourcing in the public sector

BENEFIT	EXPLANATION
Process efficiencies	Reducing time and effort spent on tendering and contract management; reduced paperwork; fewer human errors
Compliance	Eg with the provisions of the Efficiency Review and the National Procurement Strategy for Local Government
Cost savings	Reducing the direct costs of tendering (for both buyer and suppliers); more efficient comparison, supporting savings through competition
Collaboration	Making it easier for purchasers to work together on common sourcing projects across different departments and regions
Strategic focus	Allowing purchasing professionals to focus on value-added and strategic procurement activity rather than administration

Engaging the market

The **internet** is now one of the most-used sources of information on supply markets. The advantages and disadvantages of using it to identify potential suppliers are summarised in the table below.

Using the internet to identify potential suppliers

ADVANTAGES	DISADVANTAGES
Global, 24/7 available source of data	Excess volume of information
Low-cost, fast, convenient info search	Information may be unreliable or outdated
Information generally frequently up-dated	Difficulty verifying data, source credibility
Access to small, niche, global suppliers	Limited ability to 'sample' product or service
Access to customer feedback, reports, ratings, certification data etc	Supports global sourcing – creating logistical challenges, risks etc
Some ability to 'sample' product or service (eg virtual tours, digital samples)	May discriminate against developing country suppliers
Facilities for direct contact (eg via email)	

The internet and the world wide web are an accepted framework for implementing and delivering information system applications. The internet is a global collection of telecommunications-linked computer networks, which has revolutionised global communication and commerce through tools such as email, and interactive, transaction-enabled websites.

An **intranet** is a set of networked and/or internet-linked computers. This private network is usually only accessible to registered users, within the same organisation or work group. Access is restricted by passwords and user group accounts, for example.

Intranets are used in internal supply chain and employee communication: only authorised internal users are able to access relevant web pages and dedicated email facilities. Intranets offer significant advantages for integrating internal supply chain communications.

An **extranet** is an intranet that has been extended to give selected external partners (such as suppliers) authorised access to particular areas or levels of the organisation's website or information network, for exchanging data and applications, and sharing information.

Supplier access to a buyer's extranet system is generally protected, requiring defined verification of identity (eg via a user ID), supplier codes and passwords.

Extranets are particularly useful tools for relationship management, inter-organisational partnerships and direct e-procurement transactions

Procurement-focused extranets usually provide suppliers with:

- Real-time access to inventory and demand information
- Authorised report information eg their vendor rating analysis.

Extranet systems provide potential for removing process costs and increasing supply chain communication, real-time information-sharing, and co-ordination. They support the automation of routine procurement tasks and support the increasing focus of procurement professionals on strategic value-adding roles rather than transactional and communication tasks.

E-requisitioning and e-ordering

Electronic requisitioning is designed to simplify the process whereby the procurement function captures requisitions from users, and provides information about both the requisitioner and the requirement.

The database contains records of all materials and parts, code numbers, descriptions, usage records and current stock balance – as well as prices of recent acquisitions and supplier details. Stock levels are automatically updated as items are received into, or issued from, inventory, and re-orders are generated automatically when a pre-determined level is reached, or when a master production schedule (or bill of materials) dictates. Where the economic order quantity (EOQ) model is used for stock replenishment, the system can compute and requisition the appropriate re-order quantity.

Requirement planning and specification tools include:

- Integrated systems for resource planning, such as materials requirements planning (MRP), manufacturing resources planning (MRP II) and enterprise resource planning (ERP) systems.

- Design and development systems (eg computer aided design and manufacture – CAD/CAM), which may similarly generate requisitions and specifications for materials and components included in new product designs.

Point of sale devices involve the use of barcoding and radio frequency identification (RFID) tagging to record sales at point-of-sale terminals, which are linked to IT systems. Electronic point of sale (EPOS) systems can be connected to inventory management systems, to trigger automatic stock requisition and replenishment.

In such a system, data on the cost structure and current stock status of each product is stored on a centralised database. When a product sale is processed at the point of sale (using EPOS), the transactional adjustment is made to the product stock status. This enables a real time update of all stock status or inventory records, which can be used to trigger electronic requisitions.

EPOS can be used to track product sales, stock availability and location, and the location of deliveries (using global positioning systems or GPS technology). It can be connected to point-of-sale payment systems (via electronic funds transfer) and management information systems (for sales analysis, demand forecasting and inventory). In marketing contexts, it also supports the use of loyalty cards, as a way of incentivising customer loyalty and gathering customer data.

Main benefits of an EPOS system:

- Efficient and accurate processing of customer transactions, reducing queuing time
- Stock management
- Rapid communication of supply and demand information throughout the supply chain
- Access to data on wastage, profit margins, sales trends, consumer purchasing patterns etc

With **e-ordering** once an e-requisition has been confirmed, the buyer may specify the selected supplier and the system generates documentation for procurement, accounts, acknowledgement, receiving and inspection. Desk-top procurement systems generally also allow users to place electronic call-off orders with approved suppliers, within the framework of a supply contract already set up by the procurement function.

Electronic contracts **(e-contracts)** can be created and transmitted to suppliers (and other relevant stakeholders). This has particular value-adding benefits, in:

- Enabling the 'cutting and pasting' of standard contract terms
- Enabling strong controls over confidentiality
- Enabling strong contract variation, change and version control
- Integration with a contract management database.

E-catalogues

An online catalogue **(e-catalogue)** is the electronic equivalent of a supplier's printed catalogue, providing product specifications and price information. However, an interactive e-catalogue also includes:

- Integrated stock database interrogation (to check availability and location)
- Integrated ordering and payment (e-commerce) facilities.

This allows for efficient and cost-effective procurement of proprietary goods and services – especially since, with the aid of internet search engine tools, price comparisons of specified products can be obtained within seconds.

To be effective online catalogues should provide the following facilities.

- User-friendly navigation
- Comprehensive, focused information content
- E-commerce facilities, such as a 'trolley', 'checkout' and payment

E-auctions

There are two main approaches to **e-auctions**.

- In a standard auction, suppliers offer goods online, and potential buyers bid competitively. All bids are 'open', so buyers may raise their offers competitively during the auction. At the end of the specified bidding period, the highest bid wins.
- In a *reverse auction,* the *buyer* specifies its requirements, and *suppliers* submit competitive quotes. Again, all bids are open, so suppliers may lower their prices competitively during the auction. At the end of the bidding period, the lowest bid compliant with the specification wins.

The increasingly common practice of using online reverse auctions has attracted much comment in the procurement literature. Many benefits are claimed for online auctions. Online auctions have also come in for criticism. 'Lowest-price reverse auction processes should be used only where there is little concern about production specifications or the suppliers selected. They are not appropriate for complex products or projects requiring collaboration or considerable negotiation.'

E-tendering

The use of **e-tendering** replaces traditional manual paper-based processes for competitive tendering with electronically facilitated processes based on best tendering practices. E-tendering systems provide additional support such as archiving, document management, early warning of opportunities to suppliers, and maintenance of approved and/or potential supplier lists. If such a system is integrated with the organisation's contract management system, the complete lifecycle of the contract can be managed, and re-tendering (when the contact comes up for renewal) co-ordinated.

A number of benefits are typically claimed for e-tendering, both tangible (eg in terms of cost savings, efficiency gains and added value) and intangible (eg in terms of relationship development and sustainability).

E-tendering systems can help to ensure consistency of tendering procedures and embed tender best practice in an organisation. They can promote procurement centres of excellence, responsible for defining and applying the tender process and specifying standard tender documents, such as terms and conditions of contract.

A major benefit of e-tendering is the potential for process efficiencies, as a result of reducing tender cycle times, and reducing labour-intensive tasks and paperwork. E-tendering systems automate or eliminate many repetitive, routine administrative tasks.

E-tendering provides a platform for cross-functional collaboration, facilitating internal communication and data sharing about procurement projects. E-tendering facilitates the fast and accurate screening of bids against pre-qualification data, enabling the efficient rejection of suppliers that fail to meet the tender specification.

Integrated document management functionality enables secure and efficient storage and retrieval of tender-related documents. Automation generally improves the transparency and fairness of the tendering process.

The quality of integrated information capture and storage also provides an improved 'audit trail': the recorded history of events and decisions leading up to contract award.

Drawbacks to e-tendering:

- Limited access for suppliers lacking the technical know-how or equipment to bid electronically
- Issues around the security of commercial information and intellectual property shared in the course of the tender exercise
- Significant initial investment costs associated with specialist equipment, software, staff training and so on

OWN NOTES

9

OWN NOTES

CHAPTER 10

Sourcing in the Private and Third Sectors

Private sector organisations

Classifying private sector organisations

- By ownership and control – sole traders, partnerships, limited companies
- By size – from SMEs to multinationals
- By business activity – primary, secondary, tertiary industries

Private sector organisations may be formed or 'constituted' in various different ways.

- An individual in business as a **sole trader**
- A group of individuals in business together as a **partnership**
- A potentially very large number of people may carry on a business according to specific legal requirements for 'incorporation' as a **company**.

A sole tradership may be an appropriate business type for a tradesperson, say, or a shopkeeper or freelance designer. There is no legal distinction between the individual person and the business entity.

A partnership is defined in UK law as 'the relation which subsists between persons carrying on a business in common with a view of profit'. There must be at least two to a standard maximum of 20 partners, for a commercial partnership.

Like a sole tradership (and *unlike* a company), a partnership does not have a separate legal identity from its members.

- Partners jointly own the assets of the partnership and are personally liable for its debts.
- Partners are entitled to participate in management and act as agents of the firm.
- A change of partners terminates the old firm and begins a new one.

A limited company is an 'incorporated' body: that is, it is considered a separate legal entity (or 'person') from its individual owners (shareholders).

- The company can own assets, enter into contracts and incur liabilities in its own name.
- If the company incurs a debt, payment will come from the assets owned by the company. The individual owners cannot be asked to contribute to the payment from their personal funds. (Hence, a 'limited company'.)

The people who pay for shares in a company are the shareholders, also known as the members of the company.

Public vs private limited companies:

- A **public** limited company may offer its shares to the general public.
- A **public** limited company must have a minimum authorised share capital of £50,000, with allotted shares of at least that value, and a minimum of two members and two directors.
- A **public** limited company is subject to detailed company law requirements in regard to shares, directors, annual general meetings, accounting and so on. For *private* limited companies, there is much less red tape.

Private sector organisations vary widely by size:

- A 'micro' enterprise is one which has fewer than 10 employees and an annual turnover of less than 2 million euros.
- A 'small' enterprise is one which has 10–49 employees and an annual turnover of less than 10 million euros.
- A 'medium-sized' enterprise is one which has 50–249 employees and an annual turnover of less than 50 million euros.
- A 'large-scale' enterprise employs more than 250 employees, with an annual turnover of more than 50 million euros.

Particular attention has been given to **small and medium enterprises** (SMEs) in recent years, as (a) they are a significant contributor to economic activity and (b) because they require financial guidance and support in order to overcome lack of economic strength in competition with larger players.

SMEs may have an advantage over large firms in clearly defined, small markets: it would not be worth large firms entering markets where there is no scope for cost-effective mass production. SMEs are at a disadvantage in areas such as: raising loan and share capital; managing cashflow; ability to take financial risks; and dealing with bureaucratic requirements.

Large organisations enjoy **economies of scale**. A firm in an industry with a large consumer market may have to grow to a certain size in order to benefit from such economies of scale, and thus to be cost-competitive with larger players.

UK government support has focused on the problems and disadvantages of SMEs, in these areas, with initiatives designed to:

- Encourage on-time payment of bills by PLCs and public sector bodies
- Relax rules and regulations applicable to SMEs
- Reduce the tax burden on small business
- Provide grants to assist SMEs in rural areas or areas of industrial decline
- Provide information, advice and support

Particular challenges for the procurement or supply chain function in SMEs:

- A procurement officer in an SME will work within a limited expenditure budget and tight cost controls; will need to manage cashflow closely; and may have to develop a supply chain which can respond to innovation, short product lifecycles etc
- A procurement officer buying *from* an SME will need to take into account the firm's limited capacity to handle volume; its potential financial instability; and its cashflow issues.

Key sources of finance for private sector organisations.

- Initial capital investment by the owners of the business or by venture capitalists
- Share capital: that is, the sale of shares in the company
- Retained profits resulting from the profit-generating activities of the business
- Loan finance, such as bank overdraft facilities, or bank loans and debentures
- The sale of unneeded assets
- Government grants

Objectives of private sector organisations

The primary objective for a private sector organisation is normally to maximise profits. Profit means that the business has covered its costs and is not losing money. Profit belongs to the owners or shareholders of the business, as a return on their investment: a share of profits is paid to them in the form of a 'dividend' on their shares. Profits which are not paid to shareholders ('retained profits') are available for reinvestment in the development of the business.

Procurement staff in a profit-seeking firm may well feel pressure to achieve the lowest possible cost when purchasing supplies – but this does not mean that they will sacrifice all other considerations in order to choose the lowest-cost option. Buyers must look to the longer-term benefit of their organisation, and more complex definitions of 'value'.

Procurement teams can, however, contribute measurably to profitability through savings which in turn contribute to bottom line profit.

One of the key features of the private sector is the very strong influence of **competition**. Securing competitive advantage, in order to win *more* customers and *better quality* customers is therefore a key focus of private sector strategy.

Competitive advantage may be defined as the ability to deliver value to customers more efficiently or effectively than one's competitors.

Market share is a key indicator of performance for many private sector organisations in competitive markets. It enables firms to identify whether increases in their sales result from the market expanding – or from capturing customers and sales from competitors.

Corporate social responsibility is increasingly prioritised as a corporate objective in the private sector, owing to public, media and consumer pressure, and the risk of reputational

10

damage as a result of the exposure of irresponsible corporate (and supply chain) behaviour.

Benefits of CSR:

- There are financial and operational penalties for failure to comply with law relating to CSR.
- Voluntary measures may enhance corporate image and build a positive brand.
- Above-statutory provisions for employees and suppliers may be necessary to attract, retain and motivate them to provide quality service and commitment.
- Increasing consumer awareness of social responsibility issues creates a market demand for CSR.
- Social responsibility helps to create a climate in which business can prosper in the long term. In the same way, ethical sourcing helps to create a climate in which mutually-beneficial long-term relationships with suppliers can be preserved.

The regulation of private sector procurement

There are four main areas in which a nation's government influences private sector organisations. 1) Governments influence the operation of organisations. 2) Governments influence the costs and revenues incurred by organisations. 3) Governments influence organisations by the actions they take in pursuing macroeconomic objectives. 4) Governments influence the values and norms that are regarded as acceptable within the national culture.

Governments of all persuasions accept that some regulation of the private sector generally is desirable.

Despite attempts to increase competition and innovation in markets through a process of de-regulation (eg in financial services), there are increasing legal and political constraints on managerial decision making.

Privatised firms are those such as British Telecom that used to be in public ownership but were sold by the government into private hands. In order to ensure that public services continue to be delivered (and priced) fairly, the government has imposed a regulatory regime on these firms. The main power is concerned with limiting price rises although a range of other powers can be used.

Key features of private sector procurement

A **brand** is defined by marketing guru Philip Kotler as 'a name, term, sign, symbol or design, or combination of them, intended to *identify* the goods or services of one seller or group of sellers, and to *differentiate* them from those of competitors [in the perceptions of customers]'.

By developing an identifiable and distinctive brand identity, branding allows customers to develop perceptions of the brand's values which support purchase decisions and ideally foster customer loyalty. The term 'brand values' refers to what a product or corporate brand 'stands for' in the minds of customers and other stakeholders: the core values and characteristics associated with the brand.

The term **brand positioning** is given to the way consumers define or 'place' a brand on important attributes, or how the brand is perceived or 'placed' relative to competing products and organisations. Procurement decisions should support any quality values attached to the brand.

A key feature of private sector innovative procurement is the extent to which the interests of buyers and suppliers have become integrated or 'aligned'. Dyadic supply relationships (with direct suppliers) have been replaced by supply chain relationships and supply chain management: an orientation which emphasises the continuous flow of value towards the customer from first producers to end users.

Rather than firms competing, the modern view is that whole supply chains compete to offer customer value (and meet customer demand) more efficiently and effectively than their competitors. Suppliers are therefore seen as essential collaborators in value delivery, competitive advantage and business success.

Supply chain management is often used to pursue mutual benefits, through mechanisms such as supplier development and working collaboratively on mutual issues.

A number of supply chain approaches developed In the private sector have come to be regarded as innovative best practice which could benefit public sector procurement.

- Early involvement of procurement
- Early involvement of suppliers
- The use of electronic procurement
- Pro-active contract management
- Flexibility in the use of competition

Third sector organisations

The **'third sector'** of an economy comprises non-governmental organisations (NGOs) which are operated on a **not-for-profit** (NFP) basis, generally reinvesting any 'surplus' from their activities to further social, environmental, cultural or other objectives.

The range of third sector organisations is very wide, and they may have a range of different specific purposes. As with public sector organisations, the range of an NFP organisation's stakeholders can therefore be wide.

Key features of third sector procurement

A significant factor affecting procurement in NFP organisations is that they are seen as performing a 'stewardship' function. That is, they are spending money that has been derived not from the organisation's own trading efforts, but from someone else's donations or taxes.

10

Procurement functions are therefore more closely scrutinised and regulated than in the private commercial sector, with a strong emphasis on accountability and stewardship.

Third sector organisations generally establish clear governance structures for their management – and procurement – in order to provide clarity, accountability, checks and controls on the use of funds.

Third sector organisations are subject to the same general laws and regulations as private and public sector enterprises.

Key drivers for procurement policy in third sector organisations:

- The values of internal and external stakeholders which are often directly related to the mission and purpose of the organisation
- The need to align procurement policies and procedures with the core values, cause, issue or theme promoted by the organisation
- The management of reputation and reputational risk
- The need to source inputs for a very wide range of activities
- The need to act as retail or merchandise buyers
- The need for differentiation (eg via best practice sustainable procurement policies, or distinctive merchandise for re-sale to raise funds)
- Limited resources – therefore a strong emphasis on cost control
- The need for economic sustainability
- The need for transparency, accountability and stewardship in the management of funds – and resulting oversight and regulation

Organisations that impact on product and safety standards

A **standards organisation** is one whose primary activities are developing, coordinating, revising, or amending technical or safety standards that are intended to meet the needs of a wide number of users. They include: the International Organisation for Standardisation (ISO), the International Electrotechnical Commission (IEC), and the International Telecommunication Union (ITU). These three organisations together comprise the World Standards Cooperation (WSC) alliance.

ISO standards in particular are common in purchasing. In addition to these, there are many independent international standards organisations which develop and publish standards for a variety of international uses. Regional standards bodies also exist.

Within the European Union, only standards created by CEN, CENELEC, and ETSI are recognised as 'European standards' (CE). EU member states are required to notify the European Commission and each other about all the draft technical regulations concerning ICT products and services before they are adopted in national law. These rules were laid down with the goal of providing transparency and control in regard to technical regulations.

In general, each country or economy has a single recognised national standards body.

The British Standards Institution is the world's first national standards body and is now a global independent business organisation that provides standard-based services in more than 140 countries.

BSI publish British Standards and standards-related information products and services aimed at enabling companies to implement and manage the wide range of product and service standards suitable for differing sectors of business.

Standards can be used across a wide range of business, industry and technology. There are two main types of standard.

- Technical standards consist of technical specifications or other precise criteria that ensure products, manufacturing processes and services meet fixed benchmarks for quality and health and safety.
- Management system standards provide a framework for a business to manage its business processes and activities.

Technical standards can be used to:

- ensure quality and safety requirements for products and services
- improve compatibility between products and services
- provide information about products and services
- make the most out of innovations.

Management system standards can help businesses improve their efficiency by providing a best practice model for them to follow. Showing that your company, product or service meets a specific standard can also help you compete for business from larger businesses or government departments, many of whom have strict standards or criteria that suppliers must comply with.

Adopting particular standards can bring a range of benefits.

- **Differentiating** your products, services and business
- Accessing **new markets**
- Increasing **efficiency** and improving the quality of your products and services
- Ensuring you **comply** with regulations
- Managing your business more effectively

10

OWN NOTES

CHAPTER 11

Public Sector Sourcing

The public sector

A private sector organisation is one that is owned by private individuals. Public sector organisations on the other hand are 'owned' by the public in general.

Public and private sector organisations and environments are different in some key respects. The key implications for procurement have been summarised in Table 10.1 in your Course Book. For the exam, it is important to be able to discuss these.

However, differences in objectives, organisational constraints and so on may not necessarily lead to differences in operational **procedure**.

- Public sector buyers may not be seeking to maximise profit, but they will still be concerned to achieve value for money.
- Public sector buyers may not seek competitive advantage, but they will still aim to ensure the quality of inputs in order to support the quality of outputs.
- Meanwhile, private sector buyers may not have non-economic goals as their primary objective, but they are increasingly being challenged to consider the interests of wider stakeholders in society.

Public sector sourcing

The 1999 **Gershon Efficiency Review** recommended three main priorities: improving public services by working with departments to help them meet their efficiency targets; delivering savings in central government civil procurement; and improving the success rate of mission-critical programmes and projects.

The implications of the OGC include: greater pressure to achieve efficiency savings from procurement; greater emphasis on aggregating requirements and collaborative contracting; stronger focus on the status and role of procurement; stronger focus on professional and career development in procurement; increased involvement in contracting across the organisation; and increased involvement in cross-functional contracting teams.

Unlike in central government, there is no central co-ordination of **local authority procurement**. Functional departments and committees are influential, and procurement's role is often limited to advising on procedures and managing clerical processes.

In contrast to the profit focus of private sector concerns, public sector organisations

11

have a primary orientation to achieving defined service levels: providing efficient and effective services and utilities to the public, often within defined budgetary constraints and environmental or sustainability strategies. This less intensely competitive environment allows greater information exchange, best-practice sharing and collaborative or consolidated sourcing and supply arrangements, such as shared e-procurement platforms and buying groups.

The range of **stakeholders** in public sector organisations is more diverse, including funding and user groups. This creates a more complex network of stakeholder expectations, relationships and accountabilities to be managed.

Public sector buyers are subject to a high level of accountability. They must ensure that appropriate processes have been followed to acquire best value for taxpayers' money.

Public sector **sourcing policies** are governed by EU Directives in areas such as the compulsory use of competitive tendering, the use of e-auctions, ethical requirements and public interest disclosure of information.

There are some **distinctive challenges** in public sector sourcing.

- Public sector buyers generally have the overall objective of achieving defined service levels. 'Value' is thus defined by maintaining or improving service levels within value and cost parameters – rather than by minimising cost.
- They have to satisfy a wider range of stakeholders. There will usually be a stronger emphasis on pre-qualification criteria such as ethics, social sustainability, environmental protection and so on.
- They may have a wider range of activities, and therefore a wider range of sourcing requirements.
- They are subject to established sourcing procedures, and legislative directives (including the EU Public Procurement Directives). This means, for example, that open competitive tendering is usually compulsory.
- They will often be subject to budgetary constraints, cash limits and/or efficiency targets, to maximise the value obtained from public funding.

A key issue in the public sector is to ensure that suppliers are selected not on the grounds of political expediency, socio-economic goals, favouritism or fraud, but by **transparent procedures** which are open to audit and give all eligible suppliers an equal opportunity. It has also been recognised that public procurement has an important role to play in ensuring the efficient use of public funds.

Competitive tendering is used within the public sector for almost all supplies purchased. Compulsory competitive tendering is designed to ensure fair, non-discriminatory and competitive supplier selection, based on equality of access to tender information, selection of suppliers based on clear price (and non-price) criteria, and accountability for decisions (including feedback to unsuccessful bidders).

The main focus has been on compliance with the **EU Public Procurement Directives**, emphasising the transparent use of competitive procedures, rather than necessarily the achievement of competitive supply or added value outcomes.

One key challenge for public procurement is that inflexible use of competitive tendering may inhibit the development of the kinds of long-term collaborative relationships which underlie strategic procurement models. It has long been recognised that there needs to be more constructive co-operation between customers and suppliers and that longer-term partnering arrangements may be appropriate.

In principle 'partnership within competition' provides a viable alternative for the public sector, though it risks undermining the principles of transparency, competitiveness and fraud prevention. Another challenge is the inflexible use of price and 'value for money' criteria in awarding competitive contracts – potentially at the expense of important criteria such as whole life costs, sustainability, or relational compatibility.

The concept of **value for money** (VFM) states 'All public procurement of goods and services, including works, must be based on value for money... Value for money is defined as *the optimum combination of whole life costs and quality*.'

Legislative and regulatory requirements

The impact of law and regulation on public sector sourcing is broadly as follows.

- To ensure that bought-in materials, goods and services comply with defined public standards and specifications
- To ensure that all sourcing exercises are compliant with public policies, standing orders and statutory procedures
- To ensure that all resulting supply chain operations are compliant with law, regulation and standards

Public sector procurement is, however, subject to additional regulation and scrutiny, including:

- EU Public Procurement Directives
- Anti-corruption law
- Freedom of information law
- Government policy agendas, action plans and targets.

The EU Public Procurement Directives

The **EU Public Procurement Directives** apply to procurements by public bodies, above certain financial thresholds which are updated every two years.

Purposes of the EU procurement directives:

- To open up the choice of potential suppliers for public sector organisations
- To open up new, non-discriminatory and competitive markets for suppliers
- To ensure the free movement of goods and services within the EU

11

- To ensure that public sector purchasing decisions are based on value for money (via competition) and that public sector bodies award contracts efficiently and without discrimination.

All contracts must be awarded in a fair and open manner. Nearly all large contracts must be advertised in **the Official Journal of the European Union** (OJEU).

In all cases, contracts must be awarded on the basis of objective award criteria which are clearly set out, ensuring transparency, non-discrimination, equal treatment, and competition. Buyers are generally obliged to award contracts on the basis of:

- Lowest price *or* (more commonly)
- Most economically advantageous tender (MEAT).

The initial contract advertisements must state which criterion is to be used.

The award criteria that are used in deciding which is the most economically advantageous tender must be relevant to the purpose of the contract, and the technical specifications provided. The buyer may exclude bidders if they fail to meet certain defined criteria in regard to suitability, financial standing and technical competence.

There are four basic procedures permissible under the public procurement rules.

- Open procedure
- Restricted procedure
- Negotiated procedure
- Competitive dialogue

Buyers can choose between open and restricted procedures, but negotiated and competitive dialogue procedures are only allowed under certain circumstances. Subject to certain exceptions, public bodies must use the **open procedure** where the invitation to tender must be advertised according to rules designed to secure the maximum publicity across the EU.

The advantage of the open procedure is that it opens the contract to the widest possible supplier base, and maintains maximum transparency and open competition. The main disadvantage is the lack of supplier pre-qualification, and the sheer volume of suitable and unsuitable bids that must be opened and evaluated.

The key advantage of the **restricted procedure** is the potential to pre-qualify suppliers prior to the bidding process. This minimises the administrative burden on buyers and on suppliers.

Under a **negotiated procedure** the tender may be conducted without OJEU advertisement in strictly defined circumstances. A minimum of three parties must generally be selected, where possible, to participate in negotiation. Suppliers' best and final offers are evaluated (competitively, where applicable) on the basis of stated award criteria.

The **competitive dialogue procedure** was introduced in the Public Contracts Regulations 2006, reinforcing best practice principles for large, complex projects (such as Private Finance Initiative or Public Private Partnership projects). For such projects, the requirement cannot be specified in detail or priced in advance; price may not be the most important variable in a complex requirement; specifications may change over time; and solutions may have to be developed in collaboration with the supplier. In such circumstances, the open and restrictive procedures cannot be used effectively.

Post-contract award procedures state that the results of the tender (a contract award notice) must be notified to the Official Journal of the EU within 48 days. The purchasing organisation must include a 10-day **standstill period** (Alcatel period) between the decision on contract award and the point when the contract is signed.

Unsuccessful bidders have the right to a de-brief within 48 days of request. The results of debriefing interviews must always be recorded in case there is a subsequent challenge by the unsuccessful bidder.

Contracting authorities may use tendering and auction systems **(e-tendering).** Devices for the electronic receipt of tenders, requests for participation and plans and projects must guarantee:

- Precise determination of the exact time and date of receipt of tenders, requests to participate and the submission of plans and projects
- No access to data before the time limits and schedules laid down for the process
- Access to data submitted only by simultaneous action by authorised persons
- Control over the confidentiality of all data received and opened.

Contracting authorities which decide to hold an electronic auction must state that fact in the contract notice.

The main means by which a breach of the EU Directives may be remedied are:

- Legal action by an aggrieved supplier or contractor against the purchasing authority, pursued in the High Court
- Legal action pursued by the European Commission against the member state in the European Court of Justice (ECJ).

Possible 'remedies' resulting from such an action, if procedures are found not to have been followed properly, include:

- Suspension of a contract award procedure that has not yet been completed
- Setting aside of the contract award decision (only by the ECJ)
- An award of damages.

The National Sustainable Procurement Agenda

Sustainable procurement has been defined as: 'A process whereby organisations meet their needs for goods, services, works and utilities in a way that achieves value for money on a whole life basis in terms of generating benefits not only to the organisation, but also to society and the economy, whilst minimising damage to the environment.'

11

The UK government has outlined eight good reasons for sustainable sourcing, and the procurement of sustainable products, for the public sector.

- To achieve best value for money over the whole lifecycle of assets
- To fulfil the government's commitment to sustainable development
- To be able to withstand increased public scrutiny
- To meet international obligations
- To stimulate the market for sustainable technologies
- To maintain and improve our standard of living
- To improve health and the environment
- To save money

OWN NOTES

OWN NOTES

CHAPTER 12

International Sourcing

International and global sourcing

International sourcing is about sourcing goods and services from 'overseas' or other-country suppliers: essentially **importing**. The term **global sourcing** does not just mean sourcing from a more widespread network of international suppliers. It has a more strategic flavour, involving the development of an international supply network.

General arguments in favour of international sourcing:

- International trade stimulates local economic activity.
- There may be improvements in human rights and labour conditions in developing economies.
- Global consumers benefit from more product and service choice and competitive pricing.
- International trade is a primary mechanism for positive international relations and a deterrent to conflict.

Arguments against global sourcing:

- Encourages the exploitation of labour in developing nations.
- Exports environmental damage to developing nations.
- Causes unemployment in developed nations.
- Squeezes small domestic suppliers out of the supply market.

A 'trading bloc' is an economic arrangement created among a group of countries. Most trading blocs are solely about economic integration. This type of integration can take various forms.

- A **free-trade area** (such as EFTA and NAFTA) represents the least restrictive economic integration between nations.
- A **common market** (such as the Andean Common Market – Ancom – comprising Venezuela, Columbia, Ecuador, Peru and Bolivia) is the closest form of integration: a trading group with tariff-free trade among members *and* a common external tariff on imports from non-members, *and* collective regulation on quotas and other non-tariff barriers.

Outside trading blocs, international trade may be subject to barriers in the form of taxes and duties (tariffs) and non-tariff measures, quotas, customs procedures, government subsidies and exchange controls, as examples.

Although the trend is now to reduce trade restrictions, they can perform a useful function:

protecting strategic industries, protecting emerging industries and improving a country's 'balance of trade'.

Import processes within the EU

The function of the UK body (**HM Customs & Excise** or HMCE – nowadays a part of **HMRC**) is to control the import and export of goods, in order to:

- Ensure that no unauthorised goods are allowed to enter or leave the country
- Ensure that all relevant import and export duties are paid
- Compile trade statistics.

These controls are achieved by licensing the import or export of certain goods or by requiring importers and exporters to submit 'entries' or declarations to HMCE.

The **Single Market Act** led to the introduction of a single European market in January 1993, facilitating the free movement of people, capital, services and goods within the European Union. To support the free movement of goods, the customs tariff was harmonised across EU member countries so that the same import duties and quotas apply over every member country.

There are basically two types of goods, for the purposes of **Customs procedures**.

- Goods with Community status. These may be goods manufactured within the EU *or* goods for which import formalities have been completed and import duty paid upon their first import into an EU country, and which are thereafter deemed to be in 'free circulation'.
- Goods without Community status: goods which are from outside the EU, and for which no import formalities have yet been completed and no duty paid.

Goods that meet the criteria of 'free circulation' can now be moved freely within Europe without attracting duties or quota restrictions. Goods *not* in free circulation may simply be transiting through the EU to a destination outside the EU, or they may have excise duty yet to be paid. The **'Community Transit'** (CT) system is a Customs procedure that allows goods not in free circulation to move within the EU and EFTA areas, with the payment of customs duties suspended until a later point.

All goods transiting EU countries require a 'movement document' or 'T' (for Transit) form. It is not always necessary for a T-form to accompany goods; only that the appropriate status is declared on the SAD (**Single Administrative Document**) form.

The **New Computerised Transit System** (NCTS) is a Europe-wide automated system for traders to enter transit declarations (and other details, such as the arrival of goods) electronically, as part of the Community Transit system.

Import procedures are supported by a range of international computer systems. The CHIEF system allows required customs data to be input electronically by exporters and importers or their agents.

Pre-entry or pre-shipment declaration involves making a physical declaration to HMCE at the point of export or despatch of the goods.

Low-value procedure: HMCE has no interest in goods with a value of less than £600 and a net weight of less than 1,000 kg.

The Simplified Clearance Procedure (SCP) is intended to be used when an exporter does not have enough information to make a full export declaration on a SAD at the time of export. Traders must register in advance with the Tariff and Statistical Office, and the exported goods must not be dutiable or restricted.

Local Import Control (LIC) is available to those importers and agents who regularly import goods as consolidated 'unit loads' (such as containers) and who wish to have customs clearance facilities at their premises permanently or upon request.

Import processes from outside the EU

Imports from outside the EU will need to fulfil more rigorous criteria than with **'acquisitions'** from EU countries. The importer of any goods is required to deliver to the proper customs officer an entry on the appropriate form containing prescribed details of the goods, carrying ship or aircraft, port of importation, and so on.

For imports from outside the EU, a buyer would usually use the services of an import agent or freight forwarder, who presents Customs entries, usually by computer.

A **bill of lading** (for sea freight) is 'a document signed by a ship owner (or by the master or other agent on behalf of the ship owner) which states that certain goods have been shipped on a particular ship, or have been received for shipment'. The bill of lading acts as:

- A document of title (ownership).
- A receipt for the goods (in a stated quantity and condition)
- Evidence of the terms of the 'contract of carriage' between the exporter and the carrier.

Import duties and tariffs

Customs duties are indirect taxes levied on imports at the point of entry. They are assessed on the 'landed value,' ie the value of goods *plus* freight and insurance, as they arrive in the United Kingdom. Duties can be calculated in two ways.

- *Ad valorem* (by value)
- **Specific** (by unit measurement or weight).

Import duties are levied according to the details defined in the **Integrated Tariff of the United Kingdom and Northern Ireland,** which specifies duties chargeable, preferential rates and quotas together with procedural methods.

The right 'class' or commodity code for goods in accordance with the UK Tariff must be identified, a process known as 'classifying'. The importer or exporter is legally responsible

12

for the correct tariff classification of the goods. This applies even if an agent is employed to handle customs entries on behalf of the actual importer or exporter.

Various goods brought into the EU and then re-exported have **total or partial relief** from import duty and VAT provided certain conditions are met. **Inward Processing Relief (IPR)** applies to goods imported from outside the EU, which are processed and then re-exported to countries outside the EU: other exemptions can be granted for reimported goods, temporary imports, goods imported under direction and goods entitled to end-use relief.

Customs warehousing is a procedure that enables the suspension of import duty and/or VAT for imported non-EU goods by storing them in premises or under an inventory system authorised by HMCE. Companies can choose to store the goods at their own 'defined location' using their inventory system to control the goods, or they can pay a third party to store them in a 'defined location'

Carnets are important in the movement of goods both within and outside the European Union. A carnet is a permit or a form of licence designated for a particular purpose. The import can then be made into a country, or it can be permitted to transit through a country, without payment of any duties that would otherwise be due.

The use of incoterms

Incoterms is a set of contractual conditions or terms that can be adopted into international contracts, which are designed to be understood and interpreted on a worldwide basis.

There is no legal requirement to use incoterms when drawing up an international commerical contract: buyers and suppliers may contract with each other on whatever terms they think most suitable. However, if they specifically refer to an incoterm, both parties agree to be bound by the detailed specifications laid out in *Incoterms 2010*.

Areas detailed within incoterms specify the obligations of buyer and seller in regard to, among other things:

- where delivery should be made
- who insures
- what level of insurance is required
- who raises particular documents.

Incoterms are perhaps best viewed from the exporter's or supplier's perspective, as they are arranged in order of increasing responsibility for the exporter. This is seen in the four main groups of incoterms below.

The four groups of incoterms

GROUP	DUTIES OF BUYER/SELLER
'E' terms	The seller's only duty is to make the goods available at its own premises: it may assist with transit, but this is not a requirement.
'F' terms	The seller will undertake all pre-carriage duties, but main carriage arrangements are the responsibility of the buyer.
'C' terms	The seller arranges for carriage of the goods, but once they are despatched it has fulfilled its obligations.
'D' terms	The seller's obligations extend to delivery of goods at the specified destination; it is therefore liable for damage or loss in transit, insurances in transit and so on.

For convenience, incoterms are referred to using three-letter designators that should be linked with the relevant point where **risk and responsibility pass**. *Incoterms 2010* includes eleven pre-defined terms.

Incoterms summary

INCOTERM	NAME	RISK AND RESPONSIBILITY PASS AT:
EXW	Ex works ...	named place
FCA	Free carrier ...	named place
FAS	Free alongside ship ...	named port of shipment
FOB	Free on board ...	named port of shipment
CFR	Cost and freight ...	named port of destination
CIF	Cost, insurance and freight ...	named port of destination
CPT	Carriage paid to ...	named place of destination
CIP	Carriage and insurance paid to ...	named place of destination
DAT	Delivered at terminal ...	named terminal at place of destination
DAP	Delivered at place ...	named place of destination
DDP	Delivered duty paid ...	named place of destination

Payment mechanisms

An overseas supplier may not be confident that it will be paid for goods, once the buyer has got hold of them. The seller may be vulnerable because of the distances involved; the risks of international transportation; limited direct contact with the buyer; and the difficulty of conducting payment disputes through different legal jurisdictions. International trade therefore recognises the need to protect the seller's position, to give exporters some guarantee of payment by their customers.

Ways of arranging international payments:

- Open account trading
- Payment in advance
- Bills of exchange
- Letters of credit

12

Using **letters of credit** is somewhat complex and to help your understanding it is worthwhile to bear in mind what the system attempts to achieve.

- The seller's aim is to ensure that it will get paid, without the need for costly and time-consuming litigation or arbitration (particularly in a foreign jurisdiction).
- The buyer's aim is to ensure that payment is *not* made until it is sure that the goods have been safely transferred to its possession.

In order to achieve this, two local banks are used as intermediaries.

From the supplier/exporter's point of view, a 'confirmed irrevocable' letter of credit is the most secure method of payment in international trade, as it offers a legal guarantee of payment.

- **'Confirmed'** means that the advising bank has confirmed the arrangement with the seller in its own country, and the seller therefore has confidence in receiving funds from a local source, once it has delivered the required documents.
- **'Irrevocable'** means that the issuing bank receives an authority which cannot be revoked or withdrawn by the buyer (even in the event of a contractual dispute) – and undertakes irrevocably to honour the credit.

Dispute resolution

It is essential to know **the applicable law governing an international contract of sale**, and which country's courts have jurisdiction (or power) in any subsequent dispute. The Rome Convention allows the parties to the contract to agree on which law will be applicable. They may do this by an express clause in the contract.

If the applicable law is not expressed in the contract, and questions or disputes arise, it may be inferred from the nature of the contract and the prevailing circumstances. The general rule is that the choice of law should be the law with which the contract is most closely associated: generally, the law of the country in which the contractual work is to be performed.

Litigation (taking legal action through the courts) can be complex and involved – particularly when international considerations are involved. To reduce the risks involved, parties involved in dispute may seek to avoid legislation and seek to use an alternative means of dispute settlement, such as arbitration.

Arbitration is the most commonly used form of dispute resolution for international disputes. Arbitration brings a measure of neutrality, so that no party is unfairly disadvantaged by the location of the proceedings, the language used, the procedures applied and so on.

OWN NOTES

OWN NOTES

CHAPTER 13

Risks and Opportunities in International Sourcing

Opportunities in international sourcing

Why should firms even consider sourcing from international suppliers?

- Access to required materials, facilities and/or skills, which may not be available in local supply markets
- Availability of diverse and culturally-distinctive goods
- Access to a wider supplier base
- Opportunities for cost savings
- Exchange rate advantages
- Competitive quality
- Specialisation
- Reduced regulatory and compliance burden
- Leveraging available ICT developments for virtual organisation
- Reciprocal trading
- Ability to compete with competitors who are benefiting from any or all of the above advantages

International sourcing may be a compliance issue for public sector procurements over the threshold for application of the EU Public Procurement Directives. Such contracts must be advertised throughout the EU.

International sourcing may also be more or less imposed under counter-trade agreements, where a company exporting to a foreign country may be 'requested' to purchase materials from organisations in that country.

Risks in international sourcing

International sourcing – **risks** in relation to price and cost.

- Additional costs of identifying, evaluating and developing new sources of supply
- High transaction costs
- Costs caused by transport risks and delays
- Exchange rate risk

13

- Payment risk, and the complexity of risk management measures
- Costs associated with tariff and non-tariff barriers to trade

Overseas economies may have lower costs of production (labour costs, environmental compliance costs), which can be passed on to purchasers as lower prices. However, there is increasing pressure for buyers not to *exploit* overseas workers, with an emphasis on **Fair Trading** (fair prices paid to suppliers) and **ethical monitoring of suppliers** (to ensure that their workers have fair terms and conditions).

Quality risks arise from a number of factors such as the difficulty of obtaining verified supplier pre-qualification information; the difficulty of monitoring suppliers' quality management systems; or difficulty of monitoring suppliers' quality management systems, as examples.

The emphasis in **managing such risks** may be on: rigorous supplier pre-qualification and monitoring; rigorous specification of quality requirements, tolerances, service levels and KPIs; contract incentives and penalties to support quality performance; and the use of third-party local agents or consultancies to perform supplier appraisal and performance management tasks.

Time, quantity and place risks are essentially 'supply risks'. They may include:

- Potential disruptions to supply, and risk of supplier failure
- Transport risks
- Increased lead times for supply
- Risks of misunderstanding of requirements
- Problems caused by communication delays.

The management of such risks will generally focus on measures such as proactive demand forecasting and procurement planning, proactive transport planning, and collaborating with suppliers to minimise identified risks.

Risks in cross-cultural negotiation and relationships:

- Differences in language and interpretation
- Differences in culture, tastes and values

A further category of compliance, legal and reputational risks in international sourcing may arise from:

- Differences in legal frameworks
- Issues around 'applicable law'
- Differences in ethical standards and the cost and complexity of managing them.

Some risks can be managed operationally: through supplier monitoring, insurances, incoterms and so on. At a more strategic level, sourcing professionals will need to establish policy guidelines (eg on ethics and risk management) and implement ongoing environmental monitoring and research. They will also need to make key strategic decisions about the configuration of the supply network: eg using agents, freight forwarders, logistics lead providers, strategic alliances or local strategic business units (or divisions) to help manage international supply chain relationships.

Ethical sourcing in international markets

The main **ethics-related challenges** of international sourcing can be summarised as the desire for low-cost sourcing, available from low-cost labour, less onerous compliance burdens and resource availability in international supply markets – *versus* the following constraints.

- The obligation under voluntary ethical or moral standards not to *exploit* suppliers or supplier labour forces
- The obligation under voluntary corporate social responsibility standards not to degrade or pollute environments or exhaust resources in developing economies
- The obligation under environmental management standards to minimise the environmental impact of operations
- The desire to support domestic businesses
- The desire to protect and enhance the organisation's reputation, image and brand

'Unfair' trading arises when large buyers exert their bargaining power to force down the prices of small suppliers, to levels that bring economic hardship to producers, exacerbating poor wages and working conditions for their workers, and bringing no economic benefit to their communities.

Fair Trade has developed into a worldwide concept, seeking to ensure decent living and working conditions for small-scale and economically disadvantaged producers and workers in developing countries. It involves an alliance of producers and importers, retailers, labelling and certifying organisations – and, of course, consumers willing to pursue ethical consumption by support for certified Fair Trade products.

Managing currency and exchange rate risk

One of the key considerations in international sourcing is the need to manage risks arising from exchange rates: that is, the price of one currency (say, pounds sterling or euros) expressed in terms of another currency (say, US dollars). The exchange rate between two currencies is determined by the relative supply and demand for each currency.

Fluctuations in foreign exchange rates represent a source of financial risk for purchasing organisations. An overseas supplier will normally quote a price in its own currency, and the buyer will need to purchase currency in order to make payment. If the domestic currency weakens between the time when the price is agreed and the purchase of the currency, the buyer will end up paying more. The risk is even greater if staged payments are to be made.

Ways of managing exchange rate risk:

- The purchaser might be able to transfer the risk to the suppliers, by getting them to quote prices in his domestic currency.
- If fluctuations are not extreme, it may be possible to estimate the rate that will apply at

13

the time of payment, and negotiate prices accordingly.

- It may be possible to agree to pay for the goods at the time of contract (ie at today's known exchange rate), without waiting for later delivery.
- Another approach would be to use one of the available tools of currency management, such as a **forward exchange contract**.

Managing cross-cultural supply chains

When dealing with overseas suppliers, it is necessary to adjust to a different culture and often a different language.

With reference to language, it is vital that commercial agreements are expressed in language that both parties understand. It is an essential element in a binding contract that the parties reach 'agreement', and that element is absent if there is 'misunderstanding'.

Negotiations are therefore highly subject to differences both in the language of communication and in the *style* and *customs* of communication, which are driven by cultural values and norms.

In addition to language barriers, communication challenges may arise from time zone differences, communication technology and infrastructure differences, the use of third parties (eg agents, freight forwarders or logistics providers) etc.

Culture has been defined as: 'the collective programming of the mind which distinguishes the members of one category of people from another' (Hofstede). Culture is the shared assumptions, beliefs, values, behavioural norms, symbols, rituals, stories and artefacts that make our society (or ethnic group, or organisation) distinctively 'us' – or as one writer put it, 'How we do things round here'.

Different countries (or world regions) may have significantly different **cultural norms, values and assumptions** which influence how they do business and manage people. It is increasingly important to understand this, since procurement professionals are increasingly likely to work in organisations that have multinational or multi-cultural elements – and with multi- or cross-cultural supply chains.

There may be a number of **other potential differences** to take into account.

- Differences in working practices, which can be a source of misunderstanding or frustration for overseas purchasers and managers.
- Different standard working hours, wage rates and conditions of employment. This can pose ethical issues and reputational risks for purchasers.
- Different education and skill levels and emphases, and different professional qualification standards: this may affect the selection and management of outsource providers, for example
- Different standard business terms (eg credit periods, standard contract clauses, payment methods) and so on

Schneider & Barsoux argue that 'rather than knowing what to do in Country X, or whether national or functional cultures are more important in multi-cultural teams, what is necessary is to know **how to assess the potential impact** of culture, national or otherwise, on performance.'

At the organisational and departmental level, there should be a plan to evaluate this potential impact and to implement programmes to encourage: awareness of areas of difference and sensitivity; behavioural flexibility (being able to adapt in different situations and relationships); and constructive communication, conflict resolution and problem-solving, where differences emerge.

Another option is to access personnel and local knowledge from the overseas country.

13

OWN NOTES